Lost Souls: FOUND!

Inspiring Stor

Kyla Duffy an[...] Mumford

Published by Happy Tails Books™, LLC

Happy Tails Books™ (HTB) uses the power of storytelling to effect positive changes in the lives of animals in need. The joy, hope, and (occasional) chaos these stories describe will make you laugh and cry, as you em*bark* on a journey with these authors who are guardians and/or fosters of adopted dogs. "Reading for Rescue" with HTB not only brings further awareness to rescue efforts and breed characteristics, but each sale also results in a financial contribution to dog rescue groups.

Lost Souls: Found!™ Inspiring Stories About Chihuahuas by Kyla Duffy and Lowrey Mumford

Published by Happy Tails Books™, LLC   www.happytailsbooks.com

The publisher gratefully acknowledges the numerous Chihuahua rescue groups and their members, who generously granted permission to use their stories and photos.

The following brand names are registered trademarks and the property of their owners. The authors and publisher make no claims to the logos mentioned in this book including: Nerf, Doggles, Joe Cool, Petsmart, Craigslist.com, Petfinder.com, Sheetz, Meetup, Glade

Photo Credits (All Rights Reserved by Photographers):

Front Cover: Roxy, Stephanie Smith www.pawsitivelypictures.com
Back Cover Top: JD, Pam Marks, www.pawprincestudios.com
Back Cover L: Princess, Ashley Johnson, www.lovemuttphotography.com
Back Cover Mid: Myka, Pam Marks
Back Cover R: Trixie, Pam Marks
Inside Title: Riley, April Ziegler, www.aprilziegler.com
P7: Riley, April Ziegler

Publishers Cataloging In Publication

Lost Souls: Found!™ Inspiring Stories About Chihuahuas/ [Compiled and edited by] Kyla Duffy and Lowrey Mumford.

p. ; cm.

ISBN: 978-0-9824895-8-1

1. Chihuahuas. 2. Dog rescue. 3. Dogs – Anecdotes. 4. Animal welfare – United States. 5. Human-animal relationships – Anecdotes. I. Duffy, Kyla. II. Mumford, Lowrey. III. Title.

SF426.5   2010

636.76   2010902771

Happy Tails Books appreciates all of the contributors and rescue groups whose thought-provoking stories make this book come to life. We'd like to send a special thanks to:

Arizona Chihuahua Rescue
http://www.azchihuahuarescue.org/

Canadian Chihuahua Rescue and Transport
http://www.ccrt.net/

Chihuahua Rescue and Referral
http://www.chihuahuarescueandreferrals.com/

Chihuahua Rescue of Georgia, Inc.
http://www.chihuahuarescuega.com/

Chihuahua Rescue of San Diego
http://www.rescueachihuahua.com/

Upstate Chihuahua Rescue
http://www.petfinder.com/shelters/SC142.html

Want more information about the dogs, authors, and rescues featured in this book? http://happytailsbooks.com

Table of Contents

Introduction: Giving Hope

"Be the change you want to see in the world."
-Mahatma Ghandi

There have been many loves in my life, but my true love is rescuing homeless animals—Chihuahuas, to be exact. My love affair with the breed began 14 years ago when I purchased a precious, black and white Chihuahua puppy at a mall pet store (before I was educated about puppy mills, a sad reality of the dog breeding industry that is exposed in this book). The alert, bright-eyed puppy caught my eye, so the store clerk took him into the back "playroom" to meet me. This I will never forget—in the playroom the tiny puppy took a Nerf football three times his size and slung it across the room, looking back at me with a smile. Needless to say, I fell in love with "Petie" and his spunky personality. His search for a home had ended that day, and Petie is still alive and well, but little did I know, my journey toward discovering my life's passion had just begun.

Four years later I suffered a health crisis that robbed me of my career and my personal relationships with family and friends including, sadly, my marriage. However, it was through those difficult years that I gained valuable insight into myself, which in turn led me closer to becoming a champion for animals in need.

The pursuit started with a phone call to a local animal rescuer. I asked her how I could become involved in fostering homeless animals, and she referred me to a local animal rescue organization. I soon became a foster parent with the organization, and my first foster dog was a special-needs Chihuahua-mix named Brinksey. His epilepsy was so severe that he was deemed unadoptable, so Brinksey became my permanent foster dog and a bright light in my life for almost two years. During our time together, he taught me how to face adversity. He gave me courage, strength, and hope, but most notably, he provided me with unconditional love. Brinksey's light eventually faded, but he sparked a passion in me that continued to burn bright.

Over the next few years, I fostered hundreds of animals—mostly Chihuahuas—sometimes ten at a time! I became a volunteer adoption counselor and experienced the joy of matching once homeless dogs with their new "forever" families. I spent my free time at the shelter feeding, walking, and helping to socialize the fifty or so homeless dogs they had at any given time. Eventually, through my hard work and determination, I was promoted to a paid management position at the shelter, which propelled me further into the world of animal rescue. That is, until fate stepped in.

Divorce, college, financial problems—life's circumstances interfered once again, forcing me to tearfully say goodbye to my job at the shelter and the desperate animals I so loved. The saying goes that absence makes the heart grow fonder, but for me the absence of hopeful puppy dog faces in my life wrenched at my heart.

Two years went by before I was back on my feet and eager to refocus on animal rescue. I started contemplating how I could personally make a difference in the lives of homeless Chihuahuas in my state. After a few months of soul searching, a message was delivered to me: "Giving hope." Chills went down my spine. Had I been called to action again? The answer was yes, and "giving hope" soon became the motto for Chihuahua Rescue of Georgia, Inc., the first breed-specific rescue organization for Chihuahuas in the state of Georgia.

Since 2008 CRGA, Inc. has saved the lives of close to one hundred homeless Chihuahuas. Our founding principles are to prevent pet overpopulation through spay/neuter awareness and to promote responsible guardianship in the community. Like the other rescues mentioned in this book, our adoption program ensures careful, lifelong placement for each animal. Through these practices we continue "giving hope" to Georgia's homeless Chihuahuas.

Your passion may not be to start an animal rescue organization as I have, but as you read these wonderful stories of love and hope, I encourage you to think about your passion in life. How can you take your love for animals and make a positive difference in your community? With your help, together we can change the fate of homeless animals in our country. And that's hope we can all count on!

 *Leigh Ann Dickey,*

Chihuahua Rescue of Georgia, Inc. Director and Founder

Inspiring Stories About Chihuahuas

Tiny, but mighty.

Not Your Average Old Man

I'd been affiliated with the SPCA as their Chihuahua rescue contact for 14 years, and they usually called me regarding their most serious cases. One day, when my husband and I were hard at work in our home office, a call came in: "We've just seized a 19-year-old, severely abused Chihuahua-mix. He'll need specialized care that we can't provide. Can you help?"

Of course, I dropped everything, grabbed one of the many dog crates adorning every corner of our house, and flew out the door with the usual parting words to my husband: "Don't worry, we won't adopt him!"

I didn't even make it to my truck before pausing to think: "Who am I kidding? *Of course,* we'll adopt him! Who's going to take on a 19-year-old dog?" I later found out that my husband was laughing as I left—he's been my partner in rescue for too long not to know exactly what was about to happen.

I arrived at the shelter to find that "severely abused" was an enormous understatement. One of the workers hurried me into a back room where I was handed a limp, soggy skeleton covered with gray fur and wrapped in a towel. "His name is Ringo, and we had to bathe him. He was filthy and crawling with fleas," the employee whispered. At the sound of her voice, he weakly raised his head, and I felt the feeble wagging of his tail through the towel.

Ringo ended up at the shelter after a neighbor of his abusive family had called the SPCA about ongoing neglect. The investigator pulled up just in time to see the apparent "man of the house" boot Ringo out the front door and down the stairs, where an elderly woman sitting in the front yard then began punching him in the head. They agreed to surrender Ringo in return for no charges being filed (yes, you read that right).

Ringo was too weak to walk more than three or four steps without falling over, so my husband and I lined the entire floor of our office with fabric pee-pads. We set up a crate with clean, soft bedding and provided fresh water and warm, mushy food, which had to be given by oral syringe. We spent most of our days in the office, and I stayed with Ringo at night, camped out on the floor.

By the third morning, he showed no improvement, and in fact, I believed he was dying. I took the first vet appointment

I could get after the weekend, which happened to be at a small satellite clinic owned by our major veterinary hospital. Dr. Marnie took one look at Ringo, told the receptionist to cancel or postpone appointments for the rest of the day, and we raced him to the main hospital where he was placed on IV and subcutaneous fluids.

He was diagnosed with mid-stage renal (kidney) failure and some cardiac issues, but to our amazement, Ringo rallied! Dr. Marnie did some on-the-spot research, devised a homemade recipe for renal failure (much more effective and quick-acting than commercial diets), and loaded me up with vitamins and supplements, free of charge.

Within a few days, Ringo was tottering around on shaky legs, and we soon re-named him Tim, in honor of the great comedian, Tim Conway, and his old man impression from the *Carol Burnett Show*. Not only was Tim starved nearly to death, his hips and back were misaligned from repeated kicks. It's a miracle he survived the beatings, though we later found out that Ringo's main abuser was his owner's boyfriend. We can only hope he didn't suffer for his entire 19 years.

We were blessed with Tim for 6½ months, during which time his eyes went from dull and expressionless to lighting up the room when he saw us. He spent hours ambling around the house, and every time he'd pass a full-length mirror he would stop, stare at himself, and preen, as if to say, "What a *fine*-looking boy I am!" His thin, dry coat was replaced by a soft, thick, luxurious one, and his ribs disappeared under a healthy layer of muscle, tissue, and fat. When his eyes finally did become too sensitive to the bright sun, we simply bought him a pair of Doggles (doggie sunglasses), which he sported as though he were Joe Cool.

Tim's veterinary issues eventually caught up with him, and he began having seizures. We were faced with the agonizing choice of letting him go while he still had some quality of life or prolonging the inevitable and putting him through more seizures, injections, etc. Reluctantly we said good-bye to our beloved Tim. He was heavily sedated and peacefully breathed his last breath, while the vet, receptionist, my husband, and I quietly sobbed, hugged each other, and wrapped him in his favorite blanky, in which he would be cremated before being returned to us.

Tim Conway's character had a comic inability to get jobs done, which wasn't the case with our Tim. He successfully completed the task of showing us how to rise above abuse and neglect to go on loving those who love us back, and for that he deserves a standing ovation. What we learned from our short time together will remain in our hearts for our lifetimes.

 *Pat Weir*

Priceless

I was living in Concordia, Kansas, still involved in rescue work, when I viewed an email about a Chihuahua born from a breeder, who had been surrendered to an animal shelter. The breeder didn't want this baby *because she was born with only three legs*, which seemed so cold and heartless and really bothered me.

The puppy, Foxy, was being held in Biloxi, Mississippi— over a 1000 miles from me. For three days I kept up on news about her to see if anyone would adopt her. No one did, and so she was looking death in the face (via euthanization).

With time running out, I called the shelter and asked them to put a hold on her for me, telling them I would be there within 24 hours.

I left Kansas, heading for Mississippi in a 37-foot motor home, burned lots of gas, and arrived at the shelter the next day. I scooped Foxy up, and within 20 minutes we were on our way back to Kansas.

Foxy weighs about four pounds and can run and jump just as well as (if not better than) all of my four-leggers. Seeing her happy was completely worth the drive.

-Total distance: **2183 miles.**

-Gas: **$650.00.**

-Going to bed each night with Foxy rubbing her face across mine: **Priceless.**

 *Chester Burns*

Larger Than Life

Big dogs have been a part of my life since the day I was born, giving me many "nannies" throughout my childhood. A couple of them were German Shepherds, one was a Malamute, and there were a plethora of other big, loveable mutts who served as best friends and guardians.

A couple of years after my beloved German Shepherd-mix passed away, following a fifteen-year friendship, I felt like I was ready to adopt another dog. At the time, I was living in a house with a small yard in the San Francisco Bay

Area, so I decided it might be best to seek out a smaller breed. Honestly, a Chihuahua wasn't a dog I had ever really considered because the media gave me the impression that they were yappy accessories for young heiresses to carry in their purses and mascots for Mexican fast food corporations to exploit. But the first of all of my preconceived ideas about Chihuahuas went out the window the day I met Jasper.

Jasper's pregnant mother had somehow found her way into a Pit Bull rescue, where he was born. So here he was, running around with all of the rescued Pit Bulls, playing with them, teasing them, and stealing their treats before they could gobble them up. I immediately realized this was no meek, little accessory to be carried in a purse; this was indeed a big dog in a little dog's body. I was struck by how beautiful he was, with the markings and mask of a tiny German Shepherd. It was love at first sight.

The next few months were wonderful. Though Jasper was less than a year old, he was very sensible and easy to train. We played endless games of fetch in the yard and took long walks around the neighborhood together. As we bonded, he surprised me with his eagerness to learn and his enjoyment of our more difficult training tasks.

Life has changed in the year since I adopted Jasper, and we now have a new home in the country. The house sits on three acres with a fenced, half-acre backyard. Of course, when we first moved here, I fretted and followed Jasper all over the yard. He was such a little guy, and the property was so big, but I quickly realized he was fine.

There is a herd of a dozen or so deer that lives on our property, grazing and roaming just outside our fence. One day, while Jasper was busy patrolling the fence and chasing a flock of quail, a young doe approached the fence to see Jasper. He went to the fence and stood up to say hello, and she bowed her head to get a closer look. A young buck then came to the fence as well, and though I don't know what the exchange was between them, the two young deer started prancing back and forth on their side of the fence while Jasper did the same on his side. Back and forth they went, Jasper wagging his tail, and the deer skipping around playfully with him. As I watched from the back deck, amazed, the playing suddenly stopped, and the young deer ran off.

I then saw what made the young ones scatter. Out of the brush came the biggest buck I had ever seen—he was "Bambi's dad" kind of big. It was so unexpected, and before I could even comprehend what I was seeing, Jasper and the huge buck met at the fence. Jasper stood up and put his front paws on the fence, looking up at the animal with the mammoth rack of antlers towering over him. The buck lowered his head slowly to Jasper, and Jasper looked him in the eye, quietly whispering, "Woof." With that, the buck casually turned and went back into the brush, and Jasper raced back to me, tail wagging, chest puffed up, fittingly proud.

As someone who was unfamiliar with Chihuahuas, I have learned more from Jasper than I have from any other dog. He has taught me that a little dog has a heart full of just as much love, loyalty, and bravery as a large dog. Jasper is my guardian and best friend, and we take care of each other. He has exceeded all of my expectations, and because of that I push myself to exceed the expectations he has of me.

 *Sean McAndrew*

Won Over Little by Little

A Chihuahua named Mama ended up at the Linda Blair Worldheart Foundation (LBWF), despite the fact that the rescue mainly specializes in Pit Bulls. She had just delivered five puppies at a veterinarian's office after being pulled from a shelter by a Great Pyrenees rescue (go figure). Her lone female puppy did not make it, but the four males were healthy and rambunctious—so much so that by the time I met Mama (who was one of the first rescue dogs I'd ever met as a LBWF volunteer), she was absolutely exhausted.

Being a fan of larger breeds, I had never spent much time with Chihuahuas. However, Mama's gentle and caring nature won me over. During the seven months it took to adopt out Mama's puppies, I kept up on all of their progress.

Mama was very sweet, but due to her smaller stature and the fact that most adopters at LBWF are looking for Pit Bulls, she was constantly overlooked. My wife and I thought Mama would have a better chance for adoption after "practicing" life as the family dog in a foster home, so we decided to bring her home. We had no doubt she would fit in with our 95 pound Pit-mix, Dodger, who loves small dogs. Our cats are used to foster dogs coming through our home, but we didn't know how Mama would react to them. To our relief, Mama moved quickly past confusion and fear of our furry "not-dogs," and by the end of the night, she decided to snuggle up with one on the couch.

Mama loved to go for walks, and her bouncy gait garnered numerous smiles from neighbors. She was friendly with other dogs, but Dodger remained her favorite. The "Odd Couple," as they are known, benefited from these walks because Mama gained confidence, and old Dodger got the exercise he otherwise avoided. (Before Mama came into his life, Dodger had really slowed down, and Mama's presence put an extra spring back in his step.) This unforgettable Chihuahua/Pit Bull pairing helped each dog and showed our community the best of both breeds.

Mama found admirers everywhere she went, from the dog park to the pet wash, where her adoption flyer was prominently displayed. She enjoyed spending the day at work on my wife's lap and continued to fit in with our pack. A few potential adopters showed interest, but nothing seemed to be falling into place for her to be adopted.

About a month after Mama came home with us, our neighbor's cat was hit by a car, leaving four un-weaned kittens without a mother. The neighbor asked us for help, and we told her we could take the three-week-old kittens for the night and help find a better solution the next day. The kittens' tiny meows called out to all of our animals, and each one came by to inspect our little visitors.

Dodger paced back and forth, worrying nervously whenever the meowing became louder, which is typical behavior for him with kittens. Mama was also concerned for the little ones. While we bottle-fed the kittens, Mama remained on alert and frequently checked in. After the kittens were done feeding, Mama kept them in a small group and picked up anyone who wandered too far. She helped clean and watch over them until bedtime.

The following day the cute kittens went to a foster home that had more time for them. We were all exhausted and happy to see them go, and we were very proud of our Mama dog for taking such good care of them. It was becoming clearer to us that we no longer needed to find her a new home. We loved her; our dog loved her; the cats tolerated her. Mama was a perfect fit.

Since becoming an official family member, Mama has been to a fundraiser at an art gallery, gone dress shopping with my wife, and even flown across country to visit her new grandparents. She can chew a bone with the best of them and prefers large breed dog toys. Her random moments of sprinting around the house, which culminate in her hurdling over the dog bowls, always crack us up, and our cats have even learned to enjoy a game or two of chase with Mama.

Mama has fans both young and old. When we text message photos of Mama to our two-year-old niece, she hugs her mother's cell phone and says, "I love Chihuahua." We wouldn't have expected it, but Mama has converted us—my wife and I "love Chihuahua," too!

 *Andy Doré*

The Perfect Adoption

When the USDA raided and shut down a large puppy mill in rural Colorado, they called the El Paso County Humane Society and Pueblo Animal Control for help. The two organizations took the dogs into their shelters and hoped to adopt them out locally, but when they quickly became overwhelmed, they contacted National Mill Dog Rescue (NMDR) for help. Arizona Chihuahua Rescue (AZCR) frequently works with NMDR, and in this case we were offered up to forty of these confiscated Chihuahuas.

More than two months after the initial raid, I brought home a rescued Chihuahua named Hannah, who had already been at a shelter and in one other foster home. She was a beautiful, light brown, brindle dog, but her eyes and nose watered as if she were crying. She was very frightened, nipping at anyone who came near, except for her foster brothers and sisters with whom she enjoyed playing. I tried to comfort and console her, but she remained wary of my husband and me.

AZCR's policy is to keep each new foster dog for at least two weeks to allow us to get to know the dog and provide whatever veterinary care is needed. During that time I kept a nine-foot ribbon attached to Hannah's collar so I could catch her when I needed to. I was always slow, calm, and soothing when approaching her, yet she still remained fearful.

After the two-week introductory period, I began taking Hannah to some slower-paced adoption events at Petsmart. For several weeks Hannah would just cower at the outside edge of the exercise pen whenever a potential adopter approached. Her unique colorings attracted passersby, but after I would explain her situation and how to best handle her so as not to frighten her, everyone would just put her back down in the pen and walk away.

The first Friday in May everything changed. Petsmart held a three-day adoption event, and while AZCR usually goes every Sunday, we chose to go each of the three days for more exposure. On the first day, a very nice lady looked into the pen, pointed at Hannah, and said, "I'd like to hold her." Like all the other times, I picked Hannah up and handed her over with the usual explanations. This time Hannah felt something different, and I could see her relax. I could see the lady relax, too, and my heart just sang. I really hoped this could be Hannah's forever mom.

The lady, Carol, sat with Hannah on her lap for over an hour. She never even looked at another dog—she loved Hannah! We talked and laughed and petted Hannah, but in the end, Carol put her back in the pen and left.

Hannah didn't attend the Petsmart event on Saturday, but on Sunday, shortly after we set up, in walked Carol. Though she wanted to hold Hannah again, she told me her husband had said no to another dog, stating that they just couldn't afford one right now. Carol was obviously heartbroken, but she also respected her husband's wishes.

I found out that Carol and her husband actually live in Washington, but they have a small winter home they visit in Arizona annually. By the time Carol met Hannah, they had already left for the summer, but she had to come back for a short visit to finish up some business. Although she was going to be driving back home to Washington soon, she couldn't stop thinking about Hannah. She came every Sunday over the next three weeks just to sit and hold and love her. I knew I had to find a way to talk her into taking Hannah back home with her. I had never felt so strongly about a perfect match.

It finally came time for Carol to go back home, so her friend flew down to help her make the drive. The first thing they did on Sunday morning was visit Hannah at Petsmart. Carol's friend felt as strongly as I did and told her, "I'll pay the adoption fee—you're taking that dog home." And she *did*! That afternoon, when I did the home visit and left Hannah in Carol's care, we were all teary-eyed. I was so certain this was the best home I could have found for her.

I have spoken with Carol since she arrived back in Washington, and I'm told that Hannah is absolutely not the same fearful girl she was. She plays with Carol's other little dog and loves to be held and cuddled. She walks nicely on her leash and adores Carol's husband. And even though he was resistant to the idea of getting another dog, her new daddy loves her, too.

 *Rebecca Miller*

Roly-Poly Chilly Willy

My mini, quarter-life crisis was accompanied by a sudden desire to have a dog. I'm not sure if I was serious about getting one or not, but for a few days I was convinced, constantly checking Craigslist.com for the most adorable offerings. Upon hearing about my search, my co-worker, Ann, who runs the Chihuahua Rescue of San Diego (CRSD), set me straight about puppies. She said a puppy wouldn't be right for me because of the inherent challenges of potty training, obedience training, and unbridled energy. I didn't believe Ann—I'd never had a dog, but after raising two kitties, I thought I wanted to start from scratch with a baby. Ann stayed on my case, reminding me about how often I am away from home, and she finally convinced me to foster an adult dog from her rescue to get a taste of pup parenthood.

She showed me a photo of Chilly Willy and said he would be mine. From the photo I could see he was a little chunky, but that was about all I knew before picking him up. My boyfriend and I went to get him a few days later at Ann's house, where we were met at the front gate by ten or more barking dogs, including a roly-poly Chilly Willy. He was the very last one to stop barking, and I think he only stopped because I picked him up, and of all the dogs there, he seemed the least pleased with our presence. As we chatted with Ann about caring for him, my boyfriend shot me a dirty look that said, "Really? *This* is the dog we are taking home?"

Despite my boyfriend's obvious unease, we packed Chilly Willy into the car and headed home. Chilly's tail was between his legs, and he was wheezing and whimpering a little. Once home, we showed him his new digs and introduced him to the rest of the family: two cats and two bunnies. Everything was going okay until Chilly Willy decided to chase one of the bunnies. I freaked out and locked him in the kitchen while I put the bunnies away in their cage. It hadn't been more than sixty seconds, but Chilly was already crying. We had barely taken him in, and I already felt like a bad mom. I comforted him and he let me.

It may seem unlikely, but within 48 hours Chilly and I were in love. He slept through the night with his head on my pillow and quickly became glued to my side. I tried to convince myself and those around me that I was only "borrowing" him, but after a few weeks of sidestepping Ann, she finally asked, "Can I sign him over to you or what?"

Chilly turned out to be a turnkey dog—trained and ready to go—even putting his paw in the air for me when I am putting on his harness. The first time I brought home a doggy sweater (yes, I know they are horrible, but he gets cold) he basically dove into it. His first trip to the beach was amazing—he doesn't like water but loved running freely with the other dogs. He isn't the most hyper dog out there, but after having him I realized that any dog larger or more hyper would not have worked for me. Chilly is just so sweet, and to this day, the happy dance he does when I get home almost makes me cry. Finding Chilly was truly serendipitous, and I make sure to thank Ann every time I think about how awesome he is.

 *Ashley Ruble-English*

My Senior Moment

While flipping through the "pets" section at Craigslist.com, I found Chihuahua Rescue of Georgia. I went to their website, and one of the first dogs I saw was Claire. I already had one very nice rescued Chihuahua and was not really interested in adopting, but I decided to make a donation to support the breed I have always loved. The director/founder of the group contacted me to ask which dog I wanted to sponsor, and I said, "Give it to Claire. She doesn't have any teeth." My heart always goes out to the senior and special needs dogs because normally everyone wants a puppy or young dog.

Soon thereafter I started fostering for Chihuahua Rescue of Georgia and was asked if I would be interested in taking in Claire along with her multitude of health and behavioral issues. In addition to being 10-plus years old, she had heartworm, a skin infection, irregular heartbeats, malnourishment, and occasional aggression. Nevertheless, I was committed to helping her, so Claire's first foster mom handed her off to me, and I fell in love the moment I touched her.

She certainly had some issues, but most were understandable. For example, she was food aggressive, but she probably had to scavenge for food in her life and wanted to make sure she could get enough to eat. Another quirk was that Claire would try to bite people who approached her or the person holding her when she was being held. Loud noises like yelling made Claire go bonkers, and she was also afraid of storms.

In short order, Claire became my "foster failure" (an endearing term used when a foster decides to keep her charge) because our bond had grown in a few short months, and I just could not bear the idea of parting with her. Family and friends could not believe I would adopt a dog with her behavioral issues, even though she was improving.

But one of my sisters did understand. She said she thought Claire knew how much I loved her and trusted me to take care of her no matter what. It is truly a wonder that, like many rescue dogs, after all Claire had been through, she could ever trust a human again.

Claire and I have been together for eight months now. She gets along with my other Chihuahua and the foster dogs as long as they understand who the top dog is. She still has behavioral issues, and I think she always will, but you could not ask for a more loving dog. She wants to greet everyone who comes into the house and be the center of attention. She lays in my arms like a baby for her belly rubs. When she looks at me with that tongue hanging out, she melts my heart.

Dogs are individuals, and like people they all have their quirks. But if you can love them with whatever baggage they bring, the rewards are too numerous to count.

 *Susan Greene*

A Little Love: Anecdotes

Size Is Only Skin Deep: As a volunteer with Yankee Chihuahua Rescue and Adoption, I was called to evaluate and foster a Chihuahua named Weetzie. She was very large, not housebroken, and feared people, so I never thought I would find her a suitable home. I managed to housebreak her and finally did receive an application from a suitable family, but I still thought they wouldn't want her after meeting this giant dog in person. My fears were laid to rest when they loved her, and she loved them back. The family was able to look inside this giant and see the equally large, beautiful heart that resided within. *-Janie O'Halloran-Chirieleison*

As Good As a Winning Ticket: Mya was malnourished, heartworm positive, and having seizures, which would require life-long medication. After gaining some weight, she was started on the harsh, sometimes deadly heartworm treatment and sent to us for foster care. Keeping her quiet and inactive was an essential but arduous task, as inactivity is critical to prevent the worms from forming clots in the bloodstream. We tried to find different, non-active things to keep Mia happy, and our granddaughter, Madison, spent two entire days holding and carrying Mya around. The look of pure pleasure in both their eyes was worth millions—as if they had won the lottery. Mya came into our lives at just the right time, so we adopted her and have cherished her ever since. *-Sandra Browning*

Out of the Cloud

CKC (Continental Kennel Club) puppies for sale,
Males $200, Females $250, all colors.

I buckled my son in the car, and we headed across town to see these puppies. I was very excited and eager, but as I followed the directions given to me over the phone, I became uneasy about my decision to go. I remember the lady on the phone saying that she had all ages and even some adults we could purchase. How could she have so many ages if she was breeding appropriately?

We pulled into the mobile home park and continued down the muddy dirt road towards trailer #15. I pulled up to the singlewide, put the car in park, and sat there pondering whether or not I should approach this home as a woman alone with a young child. Remembering that I had told my friend where I was going and given her the address, I felt it was safe. I decided to go inside, and as my son and I climbed the rickety stairs to the front door, my son asked if this is where the cute puppies are. I said, "I think so," and we knocked on the door.

As the door opened, I was overwhelmed by a thick, dark cloud of cigarette smoke. Catching my breath, I said, "I called earlier about your puppies."

The frail woman, still dressed in her housecoat and slippers, said in a raspy voice, "Yeh, come in. They are in the back room."

I grabbed my son's hand, and we headed in. The shades were drawn, and the smoke was choking out the picture coming from the television on the stand. As we moved along, I could hear the theme music for *Days of our Lives* stuttering from blown speakers. We stepped over discarded papers on the dingy shag carpet and continued down the narrow path inside the home. I was alarmed by the excessive barking coming from behind the door, but that didn't prepare me for what I was about to witness. As the door opened, the smell of smoke was replaced with the nauseating stench of ammonia and feces. I could hear the panicked shuffling of the dogs as they ran from the light of the opening door, and as my eyes adjusted to the dim, hazy room, I could see small cages stacked seven high and four wide. Each cage contained a mother and her puppies of all ages. Some cages were packed with up to nine dogs. The floors of the cages were wire mesh, so the waste of each dog in the higher cages seeped down into the cages below. There were no food bowls and the water bowls appeared to have been empty for some time.

I stood there motionless, holding my young son's hand. The woman turned to me and said, "Which one ya want to see?"

My eyes began to well with tears as I looked at the scared, filthy dogs, who better resembled creatures of the night. There was one black and tan puppy who was able to stand on the wire floor and move to the front of the cage. She snatched the door open, grabbed him, and dropped him into my hand. I would have missed him had I not released my son's hand a second earlier. I looked at the tiny, shaking pup and noticed that the dirt on him began jumping up my arm. "Oh my God, he's covered in fleas!" I panicked.

All I could think about was getting my son out of the woman's house before his skin began to crawl, too. I fibbed that I needed to run to the ATM for money, adding that I would be right back. I handed her the puppy, grabbed my son, and weaved my way back out of the house. As she faded into the distance, I could hear the woman say, "Okay, I prefer small bills," and then I heard her no more.

"Aren't we getting a puppy?" my son continued to repeat, as I silently but quickly buckled him into his seat. I shut the door, climbed into the driver's seat, turned the key, and backed out into the muddy alley, knowing immediately what to do. I called the shelter, explained what I had seen and where it was located, left my name and number, and then hung up. At home I bathed my son and then myself to rid us of the fleas, and for the next several days I was consumed with thoughts of what I had seen. My heart broke for those innocent lives, trapped in that horrific situation.

On Halloween I received a call from the shelter: "We still have three pups left from the hoarding situation you called us about. Would you be interested in one?"

"What harm would it do to go see the pups?" I thought. I said yes and was at the shelter before they closed. I walked to the pen holding the pups, and there, huddled quietly in the corner while his siblings barked at us, sat the small pup whom I had held in the trailer. His tan-masked, black head made up about half his body, and his ears looked like satellite dishes. I knew then and there that he belonged in our family, so I asked to hold him, and this time I never let go.

And that is how Harley came to be part of our family. Despite his unfortunate puppyhood, Harley has become an energetic, loving, sweet dog and has even achieved his Therapy Dog certificate, using it to regularly bring smiles to the faces of the elderly and infirm.

 *Leslie Holman*

Little Lifeline

Epilepsy plagued Sandy for most of her 65 years. Seven brain surgeries and multiple medications controlled her seizures to the extent that she could have a job and lead a somewhat normal life, but several years ago the seizures worsened, and working was no longer possible. Sandy was seriously depressed after losing the job that anchored her and made her feel productive.

Sandy's seizures were caused by a slow-growing, benign tumor, which returned each time it was surgically removed. In a last-ditch effort, surgeons dug deep into her brain during an eleven-hour, grueling operation to remove the tumor, and Sandy hasn't had a seizure since. Every day she takes a hodgepodge of medication to calm the electrical activity in her brain, and even though she hasn't experienced a seizure lately, with such an extensive medical history, the unexpected can still occur.

Constantly plagued by a fear of collapsing at home or having an embarrassing seizure in public, Sandy looked for a solution. Her husband, Bud, couldn't be with her all the time, but a seizure alert dog could. According to the Epilepsy Foundation in Landover, MD, seizure alert dogs are trained or have learned to warn their humans of an impending seizure. Dogs might bark, lie down, or run in circles, but only a handful has this special ability, and there is no reliable way to test for it. No one breed is better at detecting seizures than another. Armed with a new hope of finding a dog who could perform this special task, Sandy started searching the Internet and found Arizona Chihuahua Rescue.

Around that same time, I had rescued a depressed, black and tan Chihuahua from certain euthanization at our county animal control—he had simply been there too long, and the shelter was getting too full to keep him around. At home we named him Ben, and once he was out of the kennel environment, his personality emerged. We discovered him to be a strong-willed, attractive, intelligent little guy who loves people, and after bringing him up to date on his shots, he met Sandy and her husband. Sandy and Ben just clicked, and Ben actually chose Sandy at their introductory meeting by paying special attention to her.

Sandy adopted Ben, and it turned out this nine-pound wonder did indeed have the special sense to anticipate her seizures. Ben completed extensive behavior training courses and was entered into the Arizona Registry of Service Animals. He's since been issued an official Americans with Disabilities Act card, which legally allows him to accompany Sandy wherever she goes (restaurants, grocery stores, churches, movie theatres, etc).

Sandy now feels safer with her little dog at her side because Ben knows to tell her if a seizure is coming, so she can prepare. She says he's her guardian angel, giving her confidence and encouragement to go outside.

Just think: Ben went from almost losing his life as an "expiring" pound puppy to giving a woman a whole new "leash" on life. Way to go, Ben!

 *Barb Rabe and Debra J. White*

Spoiled and Sweet

At six months of age, Candy became homeless when her family had to move in with relatives to afford care for their ill child. My sister-in-law, a cat rescuer, heard of the situation and agreed to find Candy a home. She circulated Candy's information, and after taking one look at Candy, my sister-in-law's mother was in love.

Candy and Mom got along great, and Mom never demanded anything at all of Candy, whom Mom said was impossible not to love. Candy could have whatever she wanted, including coffee in the morning and chocolate (eek!), too. She ate spaghetti and any people food she fancied, rarely even acknowledging her dog food.

Once Candy came on the scene, she was the focal point of attention whenever we visited Mom. She danced around, playing with us and with her toys and bones. If Candy wanted something, she would whine until Mom figured out what it was and gave it to her.

When Mom died five years later, Candy became our dog. At the time I had only had cats in my adult life and didn't share Mom's view about Candy's being impossible not to love. Nevertheless, I sat down on the floor with Candy and asked her if, even though we weren't crazy about each other, we could make the best of our situation. I got the impression that Candy agreed to meet me halfway.

Candy had never before worn a collar or harness nor had she walked on a leash. We had to slowly get her used to all of these things. She learned a few commands but was unreliable at best, and although she liked bacon-flavored dog treats, she wasn't particularly food motivated.

Candy expected me to protect her from any threat. I didn't understand how truly threatened she was until the day a Rottweiler came into the yard, and despite my effort to mace him, he chased poor Candy in a circle around me. The man accompanying the Rottweiler finally called the dog off, but the incident opened my eyes to how easily Candy could be killed. Eventually we moved to a house with a larger, fenced-in yard, but we never left Candy outside alone for more than a couple of minutes for fear that a hawk might attack her. Plus, she sometimes chased squirrels, which only half-heartedly ran up a tree to accommodate her.

We tried visiting people in a convalescent home but had to stop because Candy was too delicate for some people's inadvertently heavy touch. At five pounds, ordinary things were often threats to Candy, so I hand-sewed a cotton cloth pouch and put egg-crate foam and cardboard wrapped in a towel at the bottom. After introducing it to her with her favorite treats, Candy seemed to like it because she was up where she could see what was going on. I carried her around in it for years, walking her and giving her water often, of course. It was sweet to see her sometimes doze-off in her pouch.

Candy had a twinkle in her eye and a spring in her step. She delighted in stealing any tools my husband might put on the floor temporarily while making a repair or working on a project. When he would protest, she would return the screwdriver or whatever she had stolen and hidden under the bed.

She was truly a dog with a mind of her own. For example, when the vet wanted her to take some type of pill for a couple of weeks, Candy disagreed. Neither I nor the vet's assistants could make her take it, so I ended up bringing her in for an injection every day for the duration.

Although Candy was spoiled and pampered, she had a nice disposition. She didn't ever bite, but she would whine until she got what she wanted. Only one time, when a stranger approached our car, did Candy ever snap at anyone. She didn't know he had no hostile intent. He jumped back, but that didn't keep me from laughing. For all the protecting I did for her, I was glad to see she had a protective instinct for me, too.

At the age of 15, when Candy had had enough of various heart medications, she stopped eating and drinking. She had always done as she pleased, and I wasn't going to change that now. She didn't appear to be in any pain and seemed content, and a few days later, she died while sleeping on my chest after first sniffing to make sure I was there.

It's now years later, and I still miss her. It turned out that Candy, our perfect, little princess Chihuahua, *was* impossible not to love.

 *Sarah Qualman*

Keep On Truckin'

I was at the SPCA shelter in Prince George, British Columbia, one day looking for a canine companion for a co-worker, when I saw this sick, skinny, little boy with green pus coming out of his nose. He just sat and stared at me from his kennel, looking pathetic. I asked the staff about him, and they said he had been hanging around the local deli for a few days until he was finally caught and brought in. He was presumed to be old and was obviously ill, unfortunately making him a candidate for euthanasia.

"Give him to me," I said, "and I'll take care of him." They all felt sorry for the little guy and were thrilled with my offer, so I took him. We went straight to the vet, who gave the dog a thorough exam and said, "He's very sick you know. It will be a long road with no guarantees."

Undaunted, I replied, "Let's get started," and so began the dog's long recovery. He had difficulty breathing, a terrible heart murmur, skin issues, a horrific nose infection, teeth that were unrecognizable as such, and breath that smelled worse than a landfill. The first order of business was to start him on antibiotics to get him healthy enough to survive surgery. Then, as soon as possible, his teeth were pulled, he was neutered, and he was brought up-to-date on his shots.

The vet kept him for a few days after surgery because he needed IV therapy and monitoring. The infection in his nose was so bad that had I not provided him with treatment when I did, he probably wouldn't have made it at all. The infection had already traveled into his sinuses, which is only a thin membrane away from the brain.

I had the dog for about a week before I named him, as nothing jumped into my mind. I owned a Chevy at the time and then saw an ad on TV about Chevy trucks, so it just stuck. My new pal would be called Chevy.

With good food, medication, love, and patience, Chevy got stronger and healthier day by day. My Border Collie was ecstatic to have a little friend, and Chevy adjusted just fine to life at our home. In addition to my Border Collie, we had a few rescues, and Chevy turned out to be the alpha male of the five, despite being the smallest in the group.

Chevy was a lover and a kisser, and he always made sure everyone had clean eyes (including me). He snuggled under the bedcovers every night, giving a little warning growl if anyone came too close to his "spot." But more importantly Chevy was a miracle dog—we had him for five years despite his bad heart.

Chevy's decline started in winter, which had never been his favorite time of year. It began with coughing and struggling to do all the things he loved to do, like lying on the couch in the sunshine and chasing crows from the yard. When his breathing became labored, I knew it was time for the dreaded car ride to the vet—for the last time.

Chevy passed away in my arms, with me whispering to him that he was such a good boy and to go and rest now. We miss him so much, and one of the dogs here is still trying to find him under one of Chevy's favorite blankets.

Thank you, Chevy, for making our lives richer and fuller. Rest easy, little man, until we meet again at the Rainbow Bridge.

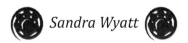 *Sandra Wyatt*

The Nose Knows

Kiwi's owners got in trouble with the law, so unfortunately Kiwi was in trouble, too. While they awaited sentencing, he sat cold, shivering, and scared on the concrete floor of the local animal control shelter, a place that smells of death and pee—a place where many dogs eat their last meals.

Kiwi's sense of smell was the only thing intact after 15 years; his sight and hearing had long since gone. A compassionate animal control officer immediately put out a plea for Kiwi, knowing his time was limited at the shelter. As a Chihuahua lover and rescuer, when I got wind of Kiwi's situation, I knew exactly what to do. I called the local animal control and agreed to adopt Kiwi.

Unsure whether Kiwi could be placed into a new home, I resigned myself to making my home his retirement home if necessary. He was not the cutest dog, but his personality, well, what a gem! He was spunky and feisty, and he swaggered when he walked. His bark was raspy like a cigarette smoker. This was one cool Chihuahua.

But that wasn't all. Kiwi's hairless tail always wagged high, and he sported a cute, snaggle-toothed smile. His nose— what a nose—could scent out a piece of cheese a mile away, and his instincts were amazing. He quickly learned where to go in and out through the doggie door, where to find his food and water bowls, and where to find his bed.

Kiwi improved greatly over the next few months, and I started to think he could possibly be adopted out to a new home. Perhaps it would be purely a test of human empathy, but nevertheless, I listed him for adoption. Besides, despite his looks, there was no reason why he could not be adopted to a new home.

Surprisingly, within days a wonderful lady, who had a place in her heart for this less than perfect dog, inquired about Kiwi. She was compassionate and understanding about senior pets in need, and she soon adopted Kiwi (now Kilo), the 15-year-old, deaf, blind, hairless, toothless wonder dog!

Three years later, Kilo, now 18, is still thriving in his forever mommy's home.

 *Leigh Ann Dickey*

A *Second* Second Chance

Puppy Gabby was dropped off and left at an emergency animal clinic by a family that was told she had parvo and was going to die. They felt they had no choice because they did not have the money to care for a sick animal. Further testing concluded that indeed the dog was sick, but it wasn't parvo. She had kennel cough and some stomach issues, which were cured with good nutrition and antibiotics.

My husband and I were new volunteers with the rescue caring for Gabby, and she became one of our first foster dogs. This healthy, happy, playful puppy instantly fell in love with our other foster, Buddy. Gabby got adopted quickly, but several days after the family took her home, they realized she needed a playmate. Buddy was their answer.

A nice story, but Buddy and Gabby were in for more upheaval. A year later the family that adopted Gabby and Buddy called to say they could no longer keep them, so the pair came back to our house to again await new forever homes.

Even though a whole year had passed, both Buddy and Gabby remembered us, or so we like to think, but these were not the same dogs we had known before. Gabby had become fearful of strangers and Buddy suffered from bad separation anxiety. The only good news was that they were still best playmates.

After several months of seeking a forever home that could accommodate both Gabby and Buddy, we realized they might have to be adopted separately. We widened our search, and Buddy was quickly adopted by a couple whose daughter had moved out and taken the family Chihuahua with her. He assimilated easily, and his new best friend became the family's cat.

Gabby has a longer, different story. Because she would immediately bark, growl, and try to nip at the ankles of anyone who entered our home, it was difficult to find her a family. We worked to make Gabby more trusting by taking her to the beach, park, and anywhere else she might be exposed to many new people. We would have people come over as often as possible to teach Gabby to trust again.

A long eight months later we received the call. There was a family that wanted to meet Gabby. We quickly made plans to get together with them and their dog, Dodge, at a park near their home. It was in that moment that we finally saw all of our hard work (and Gabby's) pay off. Gabby immediately let the family members pet her, which surprised us. Who would have thought that Gabby would ever come this far? We walked Gabby and Dodge around the park for about an hour, and they seemed to get along, so the family decided to adopt her.

As we said our goodbyes, the wife picked up Gabby and started to walk away. I will never forget when Gabby turned and rested her chin on her new Mom's shoulder to look at my husband and me. The look in her eyes was so peaceful. It was as if she were saying, "Thank you, thank you for my *second* second chance."

 *Janet Bianchini*

A Little Love: Anecdotes

Forgot to Foster: "Foster failure" is the term jokingly used when a foster adopts the dog he or she is fostering. But can you be a foster failure if you've never really fostered at all? I thought I would make a great foster parent because I love and respect animals, so I signed up to foster with a Chihuahua rescue. However, I put on the brakes before I even started when I saw Mochi, the adoptable pup with a tiny body and giant ears, which looked as if they had been intended for somebody bigger. Instead of fostering I adopted Mochi, and the emaciated three-pound Chi became a healthy four-and-a-half pounds within two months. He loves our other Chihuahuas and immediately became part of the pack. Foster failure? More like "forgot to foster." -*Tara Van Stelle*

Angie's Angel: AnnaBelle doesn't like letter carriers. She doesn't even like mail trucks, which she can actually recognize—even on a flatbed wrecker! She is scared of thunderstorms, requiring my mom, Angie, to drown them out by turning up the TV volume or comfort her by sitting in the closet together. Nevertheless, AnnaBelle is my mom's little angel. She's her guardian and constant companion. When Mom had cataract surgery, and I had to wash her hair, AnnaBelle stood on her hind legs and watched intently during the whole process. She's always concerned for my mom's wellbeing just as we are for hers. -*Beverly Gilstrap*

Getting The Memo

I'm volunteering for Companion Animal Rescue Elite Services (C.A.R.E.S.) when I receive a call from the local police to pick up a dog they had found in an abandoned home. I'm told to meet them in the Sheetz parking lot, and I arrive before them with time enough to open the side door of the van and prepare a kennel for my transport. Finished, I turn to see the cruiser backing in, and I wait, having no idea what type of dog to expect.

The officer opens the door, but I still don't see a dog anywhere. I ask, "Well, what happened? Where is the dog?"

The officer tells me to look on his back deck, and there she is—an itty, bitty two-pound Chihuahua, scared to death and crouched in the corner. I reach in cautiously, unsure of whether she will snap. But no, she takes one look at me and jumps into my arms! Her reaction takes me by surprise.

In an instant I've got her under a parking lot light for a closer inspection (it's now 11:45pm), which reveals that her skin is crawling with fleas. Her nails are growing back into her paws, she has dirt on her ears (which turns out to be fly larva), and there is a golf ball size lump between her legs.

The officer tells me she was found in a home that was trashed. The family moved and left her behind. She was living in a suitcase and surviving on rain water trickling in from a hole in the roof. Who knows how long she had been alone—the neighbors only know the family had left *weeks* earlier. When the officers arrived at the abandoned home after receiving calls about a noise coming from within, they had to use shovels to move the trash out of the way to get to the other side of the room where the dog was.

I hate to do it, but the two-pound Chihuahua has to ride in a kennel in the back of the van for the return trip to the shelter. Upon our arrival I bathe her while she clings to me with all her might. I dry her and place her in the cat room until morning as she awaits medical care. Her vet appointment is extensive—a hernia is repaired, the fly larvae are scraped off her ears (they were embedded into her flesh), and of course, her nails are trimmed so she can walk once again. When I call from my job to check in on the sweet, little thing, the director of operations tells me she is very shy, and they are having trouble getting her to come out of her crate. Would I foster her until her stitches are removed, and she is ready for adoption? *Of course!*

After work I walk into the rescue office, and the moment she sees me she starts to cry. I open the crate and she again jumps into my arms, and on the way home she insists on sitting with me. But at home I'm in for another surprise— when my partner comes out to greet us, my new foster growls and bares her teeth. I'm taken aback by this first sign of aggression.

So the work begins. In my home I have five American Staffordshire Terriers—not the breed a little Chihuahua wants to be growling at. Yet she growls at both dogs and people, and I try to teach her not to. Within a day she realizes growling at the dogs is not appropriate.

She didn't come with a name, but as I watch her walk among the big dogs, she reminds me of a bug. So that's it, then—she's Bugg. Bugg turns out to be pretty darn smart, and I'm able to correct most of her problem behaviors.

Well, the day finally comes for her to be adopted. I take her to a Petsmart adoption day to make her world debut. It's time for me to go, so I give her to one of the other volunteers and turn to leave. But I don't have a foot out the door when I hear my name being called and a scream: "She is loose! She is loose! Lock the doors!"

I turn to run back, but I don't have to go far. My little Bugg finds me and jumps into my arms, just like the first time we met. Back at the adoption center, I'm told she tried to bite the volunteer to get free of her arms, so back home we go to work harder on her behavioral issues.

Three weeks pass, and we're back at the Petsmart adoption day. I once again hand her over and start to walk away, and once again the shouting begins: "She is loose!" It's like déjà vu as she flies up the aisle and into my arms. Again I return her to the adoption center, and this time she tries to bite the volunteer before I even let go. At this point I realize that the only home she'll be okay in is mine, so again we go home, but this time it's forever.

The rest of Bugg's life was spent with me, my partner, and our five American Staffordshire Terriers. The deep love she had for me from the moment we met is a mystery, but all I can think is that I must look like someone she loved very much at one time in her life. Her previous owner must have died or been put in a nursing home, at which point the trashy family was probably forced to take her. She hated little boys and bit work boots until the day the Lord took her back, leading me to believe they had clearly abused her.

An amazing little creature, Bugg had decided where her forever home was going to be, and I guess I just did not get the memo. Bugg never tried to bite me and would turn over in my arms and show her belly if I said, "Where's your belly?" She was always kissing my face. We tried to make up for some of the cruelty she had suffered, and once she put on some weight and realized we did, indeed, "get the memo," she stopped trying to bite people and became a happy, loving dog.

 *LuAnn Rittenhouse*

The Apple of My Eye

I lost my beloved Cairn Terrier, Toto, when she was 17. Toto had traveled all over the country with my husband and me, and it was very hard to say goodbye to her. With a badly broken heart, I happened upon an article in our senior community's monthly newsletter about a resident, Phillip, who was fostering for the Chihuahua Rescue of San Diego. I called him, and Phillip brought to my house this little, skinny, snot-nosed Chihuahua named Bella, with a head like an apple and ears that pointed straight up. There was something in her face that touched my soul—she looked so sad and hopeless—so I adopted her. My vet said she had kennel cough, pneumonia, and dehydration. She was very weak and would not eat or drink. Though happy to be given the chance to help this little, lost soul, I knew we were in big trouble.

I left Bella at the vet for the entire day, so they could hydrate her and start her on antibiotics. I picked her up that night, and we began our rehabilitation. Bella hated me, to put it mildly. She tried to bite my fingers off when I closed in on her mouth with medicine, so I waited until she fell asleep and then shoved the dropper in her mouth. She would spit it right back out at me, so one frustrated day I took her back to the vet and said, "Here, you get her to take the medicine."

I was determined to save her life, but I really wasn't sure if I liked her. She was the opposite of what I wanted in a companion dog. Despite my best efforts to get her to eat and drink, it seemed like she would never come around. But one day my three-pounder finally began to eat, and I celebrated. From then on out we were making progress— running back and forth to the vet for check-ups and more meds, seeing improvement with each visit.

We knew we'd hit the mark when we went in for a nail trim and were told that Bella weighs an embarrassing seven pounds. Now my sickly, emaciated dog needs to lose weight! What a laugh we all had at that.

It's only fair I tell you the rest of the story, as little Bella is no longer mean and distrustful. This sweet dog loves everyone and is very social. I take her to a nearby fenced dog park every evening where a group of us meet and the dogs romp on the grass off-leash. Bella has many friends, with her favorite being a little chocolate Pomeranian, who is her perfect playmate.

This tiny ball of love is a complete contradiction to what I have read about Chihuahuas. Two-year old Bella does not shake. Nor does she bark, except when someone rings my doorbell. I have never laughed so much as I have with this dear clown, who now lets me stick my fingers anywhere in her mouth and wouldn't bite me if I wanted her to. She's housebroken, and I must admit, it is so nice to have started with a mature dog with whom we did not have to experience the "puppy" stage. Bella is the sweetest love of my life.

 *Carole Chufo*

Little Dog, Big Impact

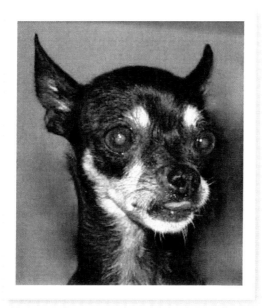

I f you had asked me my dog preference six years ago, I would have told you I liked bigger dogs, especially Labs. I did not care for little "ankle-biting yippers," yet when elected by the rescue I was working with to foster an older Chi, I did not hesitate.

Abby was a tri-color Chihuahua who was around eight years old. She had congestive heart failure, but it sure never slowed her down—especially not from dumpster diving. She would climb to the top of the baby gate that "guarded" the pantry and make a magnificent leap into the garbage can to rummage for anything tasty. She could get into the garbage but not out, so when finished she would yip until someone came to the rescue. She was unique, affectionate, and strong-willed.

I received an email from a potential adopter who seemed to be a good fit, so we arranged a meeting. The family liked her but decided their long, demanding work schedules would not be fair to her. I brought her back to my house, and since it looked like she'd be staying for a while, I insisted my children walk her. I sure did not want to hang out with a dog that small.

My attitude lasted less than two days as the bond between us deepened, and I ended up adopting Abby myself. Michele, the potential adopter, continued seeking updates about Abby, and we developed a friendship. Through Abby I learned to love the Chihuahua breed, and some months later Michele and I founded Arizona Chihuahua Rescue, where we remain officers to this day.

Abby crossed the Rainbow Bridge in August several years back, and I still shed tears over losing her. In reality, she is the true founder of Arizona Chihuahua Rescue and deserves the main credit for saving the lives of hundreds of Chihuahuas.

 *Barb Rabe*

The Gift of Giving In

I have a friend who has Border Collies. She does rescue, but she also trains her own dogs for herding. When the big guys went to competitions, her little Poodle and her Chi/Terrier mix came to me. Sitting in a crate all day is boring, and my house was much more fun for them—well, at least it was for the Poodle. Daisy was a different story.

At first Daisy would stay back and monitor the proceedings in our home. She would watch my dogs play with their toys, chew on hooves, beg to be petted, etc. But after a few overnight visits, Daisy became more and more a part of my pack. She began to play with the toys that are strewn around my house, picking one up here and there and shaking it. She would always look around for one of her Border Collie "siblings" to come and take it away from her until she realized we don't do that here, which allowed her to play without care. The same went for bones and chewies.

Even as Daisy became more relaxed, feeding time was (and is) her favorite time of day. My friend fed her dry food, which is fine, but I feed my own brand of *Peoplefood for Dogs*, a variety of delicious, nutritious blends of fresh, healthy dog food. The way I see it, if I wouldn't eat it, my fur-kids shouldn't either! All my dogs, including guests, eat chicken, veggies, and rice, which are heated in a big stewpot. They get this for each meal along with a little dry food to make for a well-rounded diet. Daisy *loves* it, and within two feedings she knew exactly where she had to wait (in the appropriate crate) to be fed. Now she stands in the crate as soon as she sees me pull the pot out of the fridge.

One Sunday evening my friend came to pick up her little dogs, and we could not find Miss Daisy anywhere. We looked and looked and finally found her under my bed. She was smack in the middle where she couldn't be reached, clearly protesting the idea that she may have to leave. She was staying right in my home where the good food is!

My friend and I talked about it, and we both gave in to Daisy, who is now *my* dog. I haven't regretted taking her, not even for one minute. She makes me laugh at least once a day and has transformed herself into a great nursing home visitor. She keeps me warm at night under the covers and is always willing to lick my nose.

Her place in the pack among my eight dogs is secure. She pretty much keeps to herself, except when my Chi (Sparky) and Dachshund (Junior) share a pillow with her when the sun shines just in the right spot. They lie together for warmth and companionship.

When I see Daisy toddle down the ramp from the backdoor to the grass, I have to smile. I watch her little, white, flag-tail wave around and the determined look on her face—she knows just what she is going to do and where she is going to do it. She is home.

 *Dee Finch*

Like Mother, Like Son

Polar came from a backyard breeder (a person who breeds dogs without having the experience necessary to ensure happy, healthy puppies). Sitting in an outdoor kennel and breeding was the only life she knew until Upstate Chihuahua Rescue saved her. Shortly after being rescued, Polar gave birth to her final litter of two wonderful puppies— one of whom is Cruz.

A snuggler with a sweet disposition, Cruz easily won the heart of Tabitha Thomas. At the time, Tabitha wasn't sure whether or not she'd be able to care for a dog, but since she was in her 30's with no plans for kids, she figured the time was right to try. It was love at first sight when she saw Cruz's picture. He had such character with big ears and a skinny body with long, lean legs—Tabitha saw him as a bit of a reflection of herself.

It turned out Cruz was just what Tabitha needed, and caring for him was no problem at all. In fact, things went so well that Tabitha's roommate, Sherri, decided to adopt a brother for Cruz, whom she named Bleu. The two dogs really hit it off, and Cruz allows Bleu to walk, bite, sit, and lay on top of him for hours. Nevertheless, Cruz still holds the title, "King of the Throne."

Cruz is a great big brother and quite the comedian. He enjoys typing on the computer and changing TV channels with the remote. His favorite show is, of course, *The Dog Whisperer*. In the car he sits with his back feet high against the seat, looking as if he is flying. His head is held high—our little SuperChi!

Cruz can be a little priss, but then again, so can his human mommy. This mild-natured lap dog with a huge heart seems to have found the perfect home. And as for Cruz's dog mommy, Polar, she's found love, too, in the arms of her foster (now forever) mom.

Tabitha Thomas, Christina Keller, and Sherri Gaines

A Little Love: Anecdotes

Ying and Yang: I had a dream in which the *Dog Whisperer* appeared as a taxi driver and took me to the hospital to deliver my baby—a Chihuahua! That's how my dog got the name "Cesar." Cesar has some neurological defects: Excitement causes him to run in clockwise circles, and he has tiny seizures several times a day. The companion I found for him, Xena, was not an easy addition, as she and I battled for alpha position, with Xena peeing on my bed and killing squirrels in the yard (no, our battle did not require me to pee on her bed). Yet welcoming her into our home was the best thing I could have done for Cesar. She snaps him out of his seizures by grabbing him by the ear or the leg, and he annoys her away from chew sticks by bopping her on the head with his paw. They're a perfect example of how opposites attract.
-Geri Allison

Love is Blind: 13-year-old Little came to live with me after having been abandoned at a grocery store. She had no teeth, was spindly at best, and despite our best efforts, her eyes eventually atrophied and just went away. Our home was her castle, and she knew it like the back of her paw. I believe that God took her a month before we were evacuated for fires because he knew the upheaval would have been too devastating for her. That was five years after we adopted her. I was told some dogs you fall in love with and some you just take care of. For Little and me, our love for each other was immediately mutual. *–Nona Silverthorn*

Some Good Years

A four-pound Chihuahua-mix is picked up by the dog catcher at the ripe age of 15 or 16. She's suffering from demodectic mange, a hernia, and has so few teeth that her tongue lolls out the side of her tiny mouth. Our wonderful San Diego Humane Society routinely visits the pound when they have extra kennel space, and today is this old lady's lucky day.

One of the shelter employees names her Esmerelda, and it sticks. Being too tiny and fragile for a kennel, she spends her days in a cat cage and her nights in the home of a big-hearted employee. Two months of trips to the doggie dermatologist and hernia surgeon fly by, and Esmerelda is finally ready for adoption.

Being in the animal rescue field has its privileges, and one is that I can meet Ezzie before she's officially advertised for adoption. Many (make that *most*) people call me crazy, and even my vet gives me his "What are you thinking?" look, but it's love at first sight, and Ezzie is coming home with me. My reasoning is that if the San Diego Humane Society can be crazy enough to save her, the least I can do is make what is left of her golden years as happy as possible.

She has knee problems, which are typical for Chihuahuas, but she's too old for corrective surgery. So when Ezzie is motivated to go faster than a trot, she holds up one back leg and her rear end bounces up and down like a pogo stick. Her "happy shake" sends her back feet right out from under her if she is standing on the tile floor.

Murphy's Law sets in: I get her to reliably respond to verbal commands and then realize she is going deaf. No problem—she learns hand signals easily. We enjoy many long walks, trips to the beach, and meals at her favorite restaurants, where she always attracts attention.

We have five amazing years together, and I never regret my decision to adopt an ancient, geriatric mutt. I sometimes find myself wondering what her life was like before we met, and though I don't like to think about her pain and suffering, I'm happy I could give her some good years.

I hope Esmerelda's story inspires those looking for a pet to consider adopting an elderly or special needs dog. Nobody with such enormous amounts of love to give deserves to spend her last years in a shelter.

 *Geri Allison*

Picture Perfect

Part 1: Getting Straight

Upon seeing the dog, the shelter staff knew that the scrawny, white puppy with the golf ball-sized head was no ordinary eight-week-old Chihuahua. They suspected she was born with *hydrocephalus*, a serious but treatable brain disorder which is common in Chihuahuas. Shelters usually euthanize "problem" dogs, so Arizona Chihuahua Rescue (AZCR) scooped up the frail pup and saved her from that fate.

The puppy needed a name, so her foster mom, Amy, decided to call her Dulce, a name that fit her sweet personality. A registered nurse, Amy was more qualified than most to provide the sickly pup with tender, loving care, and Dulce's brown eyes immediately grabbed her heart. Amy saw that Dulce had the typical scrappy Chihuahua personality and knew she would do just fine in her multi-pet household.

Dulce's diagnosis of hydrocephalus was severe, so AZCR brought her to a specialist for surgery. The fee was reduced because the operation, with the purpose to reduce the swelling on the brain by building a pathway for the fluid to drain into Dulce's body, was considered experimental. Without pressure inside her skull, Dulce was expected to lead the normal life of a Chihuahua, sleeping a lot, eating a little, yapping when needed, and protecting her turf.

Brave Dulce survived surgery, but complications followed. Fluid slowly massed around Dulce's brain, causing the little dog to circle constantly. Her symptoms progressed, and she'd pace for hours, eventually losing her balance and tumbling. Dulce's decline was a struggle for Amy to witness, and she felt terrible when Dulce couldn't even sniff her way to the food bowl. Dulce had come so far, and this setback was devastating.

Dulce's condition became critical, so Amy rushed her back to the specialist, who performed an emergency procedure. Fortunately, the recovery from this second surgery went much more smoothly. She had no ill effects from that operation and was able to begin acting like a normal Chihuahua—playing, cuddling, and eating treats.

The time had finally come to find Dulce a permanent home, which would not be an easy task for a dog with her medical history. The rescue posted Dulce's picture and bio on their website, so Chihuahua-seekers could find her and submit an on-line application, disclosing personal information such as pet history, income, references, and living situation. AZCR screens applications, and eligible adopters are given a face-to-face interview. Approved applicants are then matched with the most appropriate available Chihuahua, even if it's not the one they requested.

Part 2: Perfectly Level

Cindy had no plans to adopt another Chihuahua; she already had one 16-year-old Chihuahua named Pattch in her pack of five dogs. Her daughter, Karlee, who was visiting from college, apparently had other plans. While searching the Internet, Karlee came across Dulce, who was on medical hold at the time. Captivated by Dulce's story, Karlee pleaded with her mom to take a look.

"No way," said Cindy, who didn't give Dulce a second thought until several weeks later when Pattch started to fade. He lost interest in his favorite foods and was signaling to Cindy with his weary, old eyes that it was time for him to cross the Bridge. Cindy and her family were crushed.

Unbeknownst to Cindy, Karlee had kept a close eye on Dulce's progress through the AZCR website. In the time since Karlee first noticed her, Dulce's medical hold status had been removed, and she was now available for adoption. This time Cindy took one look at Dulce's picture and knew she would become a part of her family.

But when Cindy applied to adopt Dulce, she discovered that others were interested, too. With so much competition she feared her family would be left out, so Cindy wrote a personal letter to Amy, outlining all the reasons why their family would be ideal for Dulce:

All five of my children had their own pets growing up. They learned about responsible pet care at an early age. Although only two children still live at home, we are a close family. We get together as often as possible. Dulce will be surrounded by human and canine love.

The letter must have tipped the balance in Cindy's favor, as her application was approved, and Dulce joined her family. Dulce has since gained a few needed pounds. She is hardly ever left alone, and the family treasures her.

Cindy's hunch that Dulce was right for her family was confirmed when Cindy caught a glimpse of an old picture she had picked up a few months earlier while she was snuggling with Dulce. Cindy originally liked the picture because it fit her bedroom décor, but now she saw that the resemblance between Dulce and the dog in the picture was striking.

Though Pattch's passing was very sad for Cindy's family, it opened the door for Dulce's adoption. The timing, the picture on the wall, they both pointed to one thing—Dulce and Cindy's family were meant to be together.

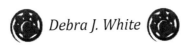 *Debra J. White*

Convenience Store Charlie

One winter night, in an alley behind a convenience store in Anacortes, WA, a teenage boy saw what he thought was a pile of discarded trash. Since he didn't want to take a chance of ruining his new tires, he stopped to make sure it wasn't glass. He couldn't have been more surprised when the "trash" turned out to be a small Chihuahua in a fluffy bed with new blankets, peeking out at him.

The teenager alerted the store clerk, who called the police, and they in turn called animal control. Everyone thought Charlie the Chihuahua was scared of strangers because he didn't get out of his bed, but when the animal control officer picked Charlie up and stood him on the front seat of her truck, Charlie fell over. She picked him up again and examined his legs, noticing they were weak and abnormal-looking. Charlie could barely walk, taking only a couple of steps before falling down. He was also overweight, which exacerbated the problem. He was taken to a vet where he would remain until someone either claimed him or a rescue took him.

They placed a newspaper ad that resulted in no leads, so the animal control officer called Chihuahua Rescue and Referral (CR&R) for help. The director, who has a big heart, immediately placed Charlie in foster care with the rescue.

CR&R rents a building twice a year at the Skagit Fairground Biggest Garage Sale to raise funds for their organization. Charlie came with his foster mom, and that's where I fell in love with the little guy. I told her I would take him home and see how he did with our other dogs.

My husband was out of town on business when I brought Charlie home, and it was our 39th anniversary. Of course, the first words out of his mouth upon returning were, "What are we were doing with another dog?" (We already had three Chihuahuas.)

"This is your anniversary present!" I said. Maybe it wasn't exactly what he wanted, but after seeing how crippled Charlie was, the love story began.

We have since provided Charlie with the warmth, love, and medical care he needs. The vet said Charlie has two bad *luxating patellas* (when the ridges providing a channel for the patella to slide in are too shallow, causing the patella to function improperly) in his back legs. Charlie also has some neurological problems. We didn't have surgery performed on him, but losing 2½ pounds has helped him immensely.

His legs are still stiff and he walks with a shuffle; still he gets around pretty well and rarely falls down like he used to.

Though he has his physical challenges, Charlie's love is unconditional, and I can't understand how someone would just dump him behind a convenience store. In the 15 months we've had him, he has far exceeded any progress we ever expected and has become a wonderful addition to our family.

 *Linda Bell*

Notes From a First-Time Foster

After considerable discussion, my husband and I, henceforth to be known as FD (Foster Dad) and FM (Foster Mom), decided we would like to foster *a* Chihuahua (the key word being "a," as in "one"). We also decided we would like this *one* dog to be older than a year.

We were no sooner approved when we agreed to foster a ten-month-old named Esther and a ten-year-old whom we have named Daphne.

Three days later we agreed to pick up a three-year-old male named Nacho and keep him for three days. That was three weeks ago. (Nacho is doing very well, thanks for asking.)

Now, we already have two dogs of our own: a Min Pin named Maggie May and a Chihuahua named Az. This may not sound like a ton of dogs to you, unless you, like us, live in a 36-foot RV.

One (there's that word again) of the things we were not prepared for was the sound of five dogs barking hysterically while trying to beat me to the door in response to the doorbell. That is just the beginning. Once the door is open there are dogs going in every direction. One or more runs outside (it's okay, there is a fence). One or more tries to climb up our guest's legs, and Nacho runs around gathering up all the toys he will not want to share when everything returns to normal (or what currently passes for normal here).

Another thing we had not thought about beforehand was where everyone was going to sleep. It seems that a doggie bed, which was perfectly comfortable during the day, is not suitable at night. Thankfully Esther sleeps happily in her crate, and Daphne and Nacho have agreed to let FD and FM share the people bed.

Our foster parent training is coming along, and not because of the foster organization, per se, as the pups are doing a fine job showing us the ropes. Some of the things we have learned already include the following:

- Puppies are fast and slippery.

- Puppies can jump without stopping for long periods of time.

- Puppies can climb on the table, steal something, and be gone before you can find the squirt bottle.

- Puppies can eat pencils, yarn, sticks, and lots of other things.

- Puppies can give you more kisses than you can count.

- Puppies sleep on your lap.

- Daphne can yodel! (I now know why people in the Alps yodel—it is loud and it carries a long way.)

- Just because Nacho came to us as a one-woman dog doesn't mean he has to stay that way. (FD has shown Nacho lots of love and attention, and Nacho is happy to have two parents.)

Yes, it's tight in our home. Yes, it's a little chaotic. But we are all learning and growing, and when these little guys have gone to their forever homes, we will do it all over again.

 *BJ Riley*

I Will Survive

Captain has no idea he was born without eyes. He runs around, jumps on the couch, hustles up the stairs, chases cats, and bosses around Timber and Chase, the two big dogs he lives with.

But life was not always so good for Captain. Six years ago, he was found wandering a busy Phoenix street at about the age of two. He ended up at the county animal shelter, and after three days still no one had reclaimed him. This blind dog was in trouble because dogs and cats with disabilities are often the first to be euthanized in shelters, so angels from a rescue group called Helping Animals Live On (HALO) stepped in and saved Captain from certain death.

HALO began taking Captain to adoption events at Petsmart, and on a routine visit to the store for bird food, Chris and Ben McKeown noticed him. Chris had overheard Captain's sad story and stopped to take a closer look. Her heart sank when she saw him sleeping in a bowl, and their bond grew as she held him.

Chris' puppy-dog eyes were met with a resounding "no" from her husband, but she persuaded him to hold Captain "just for a minute." Ben melted. Smiling, he handed the fuzzy, brown bundle back to his wife, saying, "I'll go to the car for my checkbook."

The couple left Petsmart with an unexpected gift and forgot all about the bird food. Captain immediately blended in to the McKeown's multi-pet household, shaking off his disability like water after a bath. He navigates their home with few problems, sniffing his way around furniture and other obstacles. Captain is loyal to his friends, but of course, there are some dogs he just doesn't like—he's a Chihuahua with a reputation to uphold, after all!

Chris works as the facility manager for the Raintree Pet Resort in Scottsdale, AZ, a boarding kennel offering a luxurious home-away-from-home for dogs, cats, and other small critters. While Chris checks on dogs frolicking in the pool or makes sure the felines are satisfied, Captain sleeps comfortably in a fluffy bed under her desk. At work or at work-related events such as off-site adoptions, family activity days, and community fairs), Captain captivates everyone's hearts.

Captain has been at Chris' side for eight years now, and though he may be blind, he has spunk. When disco diva Gloria Gaynor's hit, *I Will Survive*, plays on the radio, Captain tips his head back and sings along. Other favorites are *Happy Birthday* and the children's smash-hit, the *ABC Alphabet Song*. Among friends and family, Captain is always a star, and Chris couldn't imagine life without him.

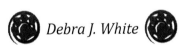 *Debra J. White*

A Little Love: Anecdotes

Ball Boy: I wasn't thrilled about another little, yappy dog joining our pack of little, yappy dogs, when my wife brought TD (supposedly short for *Tiny Dog*) home as a foster. Nevertheless, through incessant ball-playing, this two-pound, spindly dog showed me he was tough, and after a while I started to like the little guy. When the time came for him to go to his new family, I paid him a reluctant adieu, which I thought would be our last encounter. However, a couple of months later, TD reappeared in a county shelter. His microchip allowed them to locate us, and we were told that he, along with five other Chihuahuas, had been dropped off in the middle of the night. Upon retrieving him I promised he would never have to go through that again—our home would always be his. He still loves to play ball, and after all he's been through, I've concluded that TD must actually stand for *Tuffy Dog. -Daniel Clifford*

Sun Worshiper

Our two children are grown, we're retired, and I'm involved with Chihuahua rescue. My career was in nursing, so helping sick dogs is right up my alley. We have a five-year-old Pomeranian, Muffie, whom we adopted at three months old. She is our third Pomie and the only dog we planned to have, but after dog-sitting for a neighbor, we realized Muffie loved having a playmate. Lovie, a nine-year-old long-coat Chihuahua, was retired from breeding at age five, and since I already knew and liked Lovie, we adopted her, too.

Dori, an elderly, smooth-coat Chihuahua, who was found wandering the streets of a town near Seattle, ended up in our home after her Chihuahua Rescue and Referral foster mom had a heart attack. When I first met Dori, she looked like a skeleton and had frequent, intense coughing episodes. Seeing her so sick just broke my heart, and I didn't think she would last more than a couple of weeks. I constantly checked to make sure Dori was still breathing, and I took her to the vet as soon as I could. I had been listening to her lungs to check for fluid, which I could barely hear over her loud heart murmur. She did not have any symptoms of fluid in her lungs or congenital heart failure, but the vet did a chest x-ray to be sure. He confirmed that she had a grade 6/6 heart murmur (meaning it was extremely loud), arthritis, and some kidney failure.

Dori was between 12 and 14 years old, but it was tough to say exactly because she had no teeth. She appeared depressed, sleeping all day except to potty and eat, and I'm sure the coughing just wore her out. If she hadn't started improving, I wouldn't have wanted to prolong her suffering, but luckily we did not have to make any tough decisions at that time because she was clearly on the mend. Changing her medications improved the cough, adding glucosamine and Metacam to her regimen helped her arthritis, and providing higher quality food increased her appetite.

Though her health was improving, Dori still had fear issues to conquer. For three months she avoided my husband, and for a time she also ran from me, cowering as though I were about to hit her whenever I'd try to pick her up. Everything seemed to scare Dori, so I kept her in my computer room and took her out to potty in a small pen on a leash. Slowly she explored the house, learned how to use the dog door, and started coming when I called her. My husband quit trying to win her over, until one day she came to him when he was watching TV in his recliner. She would only go so close, but we could tell she was starting to trust him. Our other two dogs would watch TV in his lap, which helped assure Dori that my husband was okay. Dori eventually learned to like everyone except kids, which is fine since we don't have grandchildren.

Dori finally put on weight to reach a healthy five pounds. We nicknamed her our "Hunky-Dori" because she loved her food so much. She became a little spunky after we had had her for five months, and when we left for our winter home in Arizona, Dori surprised us by taking instantly to motor home travel. Upon arriving at our Arizona home, I was relieved to see her running around, sniffing, and exploring with Muffie and Lovie, "the girls." She loved the sun and quickly found the sun spot the dogs used. If we couldn't find Dori, she would be napping there.

Dori thrived all winter but did have another bad week of coughing. Our Arizona vet surmised that her problem was more her trachea than her heart, so I had to make sure that her clothing was loose around the neck. This sensitive trachea is typical of small dogs and is the reason why they should only wear a harness instead of a collar. In addition to taking care not to put pressure on her neck, we gave Dori a smidgeon of children's cough medication, which helped with the coughing a lot.

For 19 months Dori thrived with us, zipping in and out of the dog door, wagging her tail, prancing around, and playing. She only occasionally walked slowly like an elderly dog. She barked when the doorbell rang and recognized friends who came over, so she had fairly good hearing and eyesight. She always kept a close eye on me, and after a time became very attached.

Until the end, Dori looked like a different dog than the emaciated one we first encountered. Regrettably, when her ailments began to make her suffer, we did eventually have to make the difficult decision to help Dori over the Rainbow Bridge. I held her and comforted her while she made the transition. Losing a pet is always hard, but the joy that comes with helping one of God's creatures to have a nice life helps soothe the pain associated with her loss.

 *Paula Blanchard*

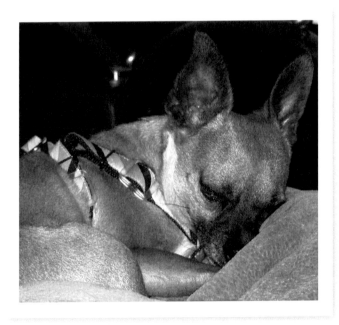

This is a story that still haunts the members of Arizona Chihuahua Rescue (AZCR) to this day. It all started in mid-March when the president of AZCR sent an e-mail to our members, stating she had been contacted by the Southern Arizona Humane Society, which needed help with some of the 100 dogs confiscated from a Southern Arizona breeder-gone-bad situation. Our rescue agreed to help with 50 dogs even though we hadn't a clue where we would put them.

We were told not to talk about the story except within our group. They also informed us that the Humane Society was going back for up to 400 more dogs as soon as they could get the warrant. About 36 hours later, five of our members headed to Tucson in four vehicles to pick up our 50 dogs. The warrant had been served that day, and it turned out there weren't 400 more dogs—there were over 600 more! So the first day we came back to Phoenix with 80 or 90 dogs, some giving birth as our transport team was en route. A week or so later, two of our members returned to Tucson for more dogs. Ten days went by, and we made another trip. In all we rescued 162 dogs!

I fostered a little, black and white, eight-month-old Japanese Chin-mix, whom I named Annie. Annie was young and carefree with no fears, but she was sick with kennel cough and *Giardia* (an infection caused by parasites), so we had to have her treated. Within a month Annie was healthy and was subsequently adopted by a wonderful family that adores her.

I also fostered a two-year-old, deep red, male Chihuahua, whom my son named Fonzie. Poor Fonzie was beside himself with fear—he hid for three weeks under blankets and pillows just to get away from people. Even so, Fonzie (now Isiah) eventually came around and was adopted by a great lady, who has all his fears locked away. He adores his mom and loves going places with her. He even swims with her, which amazes me because I thought he would never conquer any of his fears, let alone go swimming! That dog sure did prove me wrong.

A few days later, I took in a four-year-old, brown and white, male Chihuahua, whom we named King Henry. King Henry was just as scared as Fonzie, so we put him in a different foster home where he could receive more one-on-one attention. King Henry became a great guy who did find his forever family a year later.

Finally, there was a two-year-old, tan, male Chihuahua with a black muzzle, whom I named Atlas because his fears caused him to think he had to take on the world. Atlas was adopted, but that family decided his emotional issues were more than they could handle. Don't be sad for Atlas, though, he won my heart and is now spoiled rotten and well-loved in my home, his *forever* home!

Like these four dogs, most dogs from the raids have found happiness in loving homes. But as is to be expected, some from the raid have not. They remain in foster care, trying to overcome their fears, still learning to trust that most humans are not so bad. We remain hopeful for their full recovery. The most unfortunate dogs were lost, but we continue to hold them in our hearts.

The Southern Arizona raid is something we'll never forget. We're glad we could save some of the dogs who had suffered so badly, but they never should have had to suffer like that in the first place. The three people who perpetrated this atrocity were charged and prosecuted, but that will not bring back the dogs who died as a result of their neglect and cruelty.

 *Jennifer Prentice*

The Surprise Inside

The moment I heard about the puppy mill/hoarding bust in Arizona, I knew I would have one of the rescued dogs. Authorities had found 800 suffering, toy breed dogs, neglected and living in squalor, in a triple-wide mobile home. Many were giving birth as animal control quickly whisked them away, and several had severe injuries like paws chewed off from fights. Their living space appeared to be indoor plastic crates crammed with dogs or equally crowded outdoor pens.

The Arizona shelter simply did not have the capacity to accommodate such a huge influx of dogs, so the Marin

Humane Society in California stepped in with "Operation Tiny Teacup," a rescue effort to pick up several hundred of these little passengers and relocate them to California to find forever homes.

I already had two Chihuahuas: an older girl named Smidge, and younger girl named Tidbit. Tidbit needed a younger playmate, as Smidge preferred sleeping away the days. The timing was perfect, and the Marin Humane Society was only an hour away, so I submitted an application to adopt one of the "Operation Tiny Teacup" dogs. To my surprise, the waiting list was in the hundreds! This was good news for the dogs, but bad news for me.

A week later I received word that there were a few remaining special-needs dogs for whom the shelter was hand-picking homes. These dogs were extremely under-socialized—not surprising since they had been raised with very little human contact—and their new people-filled environment was causing them tremendous stress. Because I had been in the animal care industry for so long and am knowledgeable about working with dogs with unique issues and temperaments, the shelter staff was willing to consider me as a potential adopter.

The adoption counselor had a particular dog in mind for me, a little Chihuahua named Rosey, whom I went to meet the next day. Rosey was a shaking, four-pound ball of blonde fur, and I was in love. When I picked her up, she buried her head in my arm, and instantly I knew Rosey, now Olive, would be coming home with me.

Olive spent our first month together hiding under my couch. I fed her under the couch, put potty pads under the couch, and gave her treats under the couch. Finally she started feeling a bit more adventurous and would poke her little head out to see what was going on in the world around her. I was always careful not to push her too fast and let all interactions be on her terms. When she was feeling a bit bolder, I took her to a panel of behaviorists to evaluate her and advise me on the best ways to help her relax. That appointment was the beginning of my long journey of helping to heal Olive's emotional scars, so she could have the quality life she deserved.

I soon learned that Olive's quirky behaviors are common among puppy mill dogs. These dogs, who are stuffed into very small cages with other dogs and only given minimal human contact, get the equivalent of *Post Traumatic Stress Disorder* and will often have funny little triggers that send them into high-stress mode. For Olive, the sound of plastic being scraped (like soup being stirred in a plastic container) sent her into a frenzy, from which it took her up to 20 minutes to recover. I often wondered if it was because the sound was strikingly similar to nails on the side of a plastic crate (which I am sure she heard frequently in her former environment). She also was severely *copraphagic*, meaning she constantly ate her own feces. This is common with mill dogs because they often have to compete with many other dogs for food. When dogs don't receive adequate nutrition, they are likely to eat their stool to try and get it the second time around.

Ordinary experiences were extraordinary for Olive, since she had only seen the inside of a mobile home her whole life. She found the television fascinating—staring intently at it while tilting her little head from side to side in the inquisitive way dogs do when they are listening. On the other hand, cars absolutely terrified her, and I had to work very slowly to get her used to car rides.

I have now had Olive for a year and have seen an amazing transformation. Just as some olives are hiding tasty pimientos in their center, my shivering, terrified Olive had a playful, outgoing dog stashed inside! She loves nothing more than to cuddle with me in bed, solicit belly rubs, and keep my elderly dog, Smidge, on her toes. She has brought a warmth and playfulness to my household that was never there before. From her dismal beginnings to her amazing recovery, she is a shining example of the resilience and forgiveness that is the true nature of a dog.

 *Jessica Stout*

A Better Bugg

I t was a Friday morning when the local humane society called about a little girl needing critical care. Could I possibly go pick her up? *Sure!* I went during my lunch break, and as the shelter staff readied her paperwork so I could get back to my office, they mentioned another Chihuahua needing foster care. I ended up taking him, too, and so began the story of my miracle baby.

This tiny, male, brown and black brindle-colored Chihuahua was found as a stray on the streets of South Phoenix just after Christmas. The temperature was very cold at night, and this four-pound dog was freezing. When I picked him up, he had an upper respiratory infection and an extreme case of demodetic mange, which gave him a crusty "saddle" across his shoulders and back. Additionally he smelled to high Heaven.

I brought the two dogs back to my office to spend the afternoon with me. My co-workers and I played with the little boy and decided to call him Bugg for two reasons: He was as cute as a bug and surely just covered with them! I noticed that sometimes Bugg would stumble as he ran after the toy I had tossed and wasn't always steady on his feet. As the afternoon wore on, he started stumbling more and more and then began bumping into the desk or the trash can. I picked him up to calm and reassure him, but he simply couldn't sit still in my lap; he just constantly wiggled. When I set him back down, he'd just aimlessly wander until bumping into something, at which time he'd turn and wander some more. It was heartbreaking! Thank goodness I had planned a vet visit for the moment I was finished with work.

I arrived at the vet's office around 4:30 that afternoon. The doctor looked Bugg over and reaffirmed that he had a bad case of mange, but we were all more concerned about Bugg's neurological state. He couldn't stop twitching, and in only four hours, he'd gone completely blind. His eyes were cloudy, and the vet could barely see his retinas. After giving Bugg some fluids and antibiotics, the vet told us to go home and rest. I asked if I should continue the Ivermectin anti-parasitic medication the humane society had started Bugg on for the mange. "He was given Ivermectin?" the vet asked.

I said, "Yes, he has been on Ivermectin, has been neutered, and was given his DHPP and rabies shots."

"*Stop the Ivermectin!*" cried the vet.

I took Bugg home and turned the bathroom into his hospital room. I laid papers, made him a bed out of a blanket, and set out food and water, although I couldn't imagine he'd find it in his stupor. I hoped he'd wear himself out with all his wandering and find his bed for the night. I checked on him several times before I went to bed and didn't see an improvement, but he wasn't getting worse either. I said goodnight and prayed for him to recover.

I awoke early the next morning, Saturday, and immediately went to check in on Bugg. I found him crumpled on the floor, not on his blanket. His feet faced one direction, his nose the other. Panicked, I slowly reached out to touch him and found he was cold as stone! My heart sank, and I thought "Oh, no, Bugg is *dead!*" But then he twitched ever so slightly. I scooped him up, put him inside my nightgown right next to my heart, and wrapped him up in my robe. I had to warm him up, so I sat and rocked him and cooed encouragement for a couple of hours until the rest of the world woke up. I saw no improvement, but at least he was breathing.

I rushed him back to the vet as soon as I could, but they didn't have any encouraging words. The vet thought he was probably in end-stage distemper and there really wasn't anything to be done. If he survived, he'd probably have neurological symptoms for the rest of his life. I was told to take him home, keep him warm, and push oral fluids whenever I could. As bad as this news was, it was better than what I had expected. I had feared I would be going home from the vet's office alone, but there was Bugg, collapsed in the seat next to me.

I took Bugg back to his "hospital room" and set up a heat lamp for him. With the room toasty warm and a much smaller kennel to keep him from wandering, I hoped he would get some rest. He was sick beyond wandering anyway, but at least I knew he'd be where I left him the next time I came in.

I gave him two or three milliliters of water through a small oral syringe every hour throughout the day and evening, but he never even opened his eyes or lifted his head. When it was time for me to go to sleep, I said goodnight again and tearfully headed for bed.

Sunday morning I awoke with a feeling of dread. I padded down the hall to Bugg's bathroom, fearing what I might find, but when I arrived I absolutely couldn't believe my eyes. He was sitting up, looking at me, and wanting me to open his crate! I grabbed him and hugged him and danced down the hall to take him outside. His eyes were still foggy, but he was alive! I decided a blind dog was way better than a dead one.

I took Bugg back to the vet's office on Monday morning to show them how well he was doing. As we sat in the waiting room, several yards away one of the exam room doors opened, and Bugg barked at the dog coming out. He could *see*! Not only was he getting his strength back, but his vision was improving as well.

Bugg had to return to the vet's office weekly for his "spa days" (mange dips) over the next six weeks, but he continued to improve and get stronger. He loved to play with his foster brothers and sisters and proved to be a beautiful little dog when his fur finally filled in. Both he and the other little girl I picked up from the humane society that day were eventually adopted, with Bugg moving into his new home on the very evening of his final "spa day."

"Harley-Bugg" is now happy, healthy, and living nearby, and I even got to babysit him when his new parents went out of town. What a treat!

 *Rebecca Miller*

Bottomless Belly, Limitless Love

I t's probably best to start Cricket's story at the end so as to have an actual happy ending. Yes, I think that's how she'd want it told.

This past summer my husband and I were heading out of town to celebrate our 20th wedding anniversary. I was excited as I went to bed that night and eager for morning to arrive, so we could get on the road. I couldn't have imagined it would be the last night I'd ever spend with my girl, Cricket. Even though she'd made it to the advanced age of 17 and had certainly had her share of medical issues, she was still a happy little gal.

But suddenly, there we were at the end. In the wee hours of the morning, with no time to prepare my heart, she was leaving me. I was fortunate enough to be with her when she slipped away, but as I held her aging, little body for the last time, quietly telling her that she was my special girl and weeping into her fur, I knew my home would never be the same. As painful as it was for me, clearly she was tired and needed to go. She seemed at peace with her own passing, but after being blessed with this wee life force for seven years, I was going to have a lot of adjusting to do.

But let's go back to the beginning, so we can get to that happy ending. Even though we already had four dogs, my husband made the mistake of asking me what I wanted for our 13th wedding anniversary, and I replied, "A Chihuahua." He promptly told me to think of something else, so like any *good* wife would, I instead busied myself finding just the right one. A phone conversation with a rescue friend revealed that she was fostering a wonderful little Chi-Chi, and after one look at the pup's photo on Petfinder.com, I knew without question she was the one.

I was immediately in love, but when I showed her picture to everyone else their response was the same: "Why would you want that dog? She's ten years old, fat, and not very cute."

What? This dog was adorable! Ten years old, *so what?* Well, never one to be easily swayed by the masses, I arranged to meet Cricket, and before I knew it, she was standing on a table in front of me, running over to give me my first kiss, smiling her cuter-than-cute smile. I had found my very first Chihuahua.

I asked about her background, but there wasn't much to learn. She'd been surrendered to the pound by her previous owners, and other than leaving her name and age, they gave no additional info. They had called her Prissy, but there was *nothing* prissy about this tiny tank of a dog. I decided an all around fresh start was just what she needed, which included a new name. Although she was built like a watermelon on two-inch legs, this dog was impressively agile, hopping around like a youngster. "Cricket" suited her perfectly.

Obviously Cricket loved eating, a little too much. She didn't think it was a problem, but we knew differently, and my days of free-feeding quickly became a thing of the past. If anything hit the floor that might pass as edible, she immediately consumed it. She also enjoyed the occasional non-food item—a napkin with just the hint food was as good as the real deal. Better to eat first and ask questions later, right? Once I discovered she'd snuck out the doggie door in the middle of the night to feast on a fig tree. (Apparently some late-night cravings just can't be ignored.) The happy dance that ensued at the mere possibility of a treat was hilarious.

At my sister's house, we learned that muffin-carrying children and insatiably-hungry dogs don't mix. Once she got a muffin the size of a small country from one of the children and tried to dive behind the TV to enjoy it before she was spotted. Too late! After thoroughly dusting the underside the TV stand with my entire upper body, I finally retrieved the muffin-snatcher, but regrettably I was too late—the muffin was long gone. Maybe "Hoover" would have been a more appropriate name?

Cricket entertained me every day. Her "moonwalk" would have impressed Michael Jackson himself. She would come up with strange "blips," like having a completely different bark, just for a day. Sleep was even a celebration, as I'd glance over to find her lying there, eyes shut and tail wagging.

While all my other dogs were complete fools in the car, Cricket was the perfect travel companion. The other dogs would roam frantically or wail in their crates, but Cricket instead just sat in the passenger seat enjoying the ride. The very hint of going bye-bye was reason to rejoice with a new happy dance and a huge smile.

Cricket touched everyone's hearts and no one was ever a stranger. My sister's children loved her, and vendors at our local flea market always saved special treats for her or wanted to introduce her to someone. Cricket greeted all newcomers as if they were long lost friends whose absence had been deeply felt. Looking back I regret not helping her to become a therapy dog because she would have been wonderful in that role.

Cricket was a gift to me in a myriad of ways. Yes, she was an anniversary present, but the joy she took in the simple act of living was infectious—truly the greatest gift. She lived in the moment as most dogs do, a concept humans are seldom able to master. Always willing to give and accept love, affection, comfort, and happiness, Cricket needed nothing more. Well, okay, maybe the occasional treat.

 *Donna Little*

A Little Love: Anecdotes

No Problems Here: Our first rescue dog, Lowell, had been returned to the New York Humane Society twice because of his aggressive personality. We were told one adopter couldn't sleep in her bed for a week because he wouldn't let her near it, but he didn't bring his issues to our home. Our second dog, Marley, was a nervous wreck until our third dog, Clarence (who at six months old was found in a garbage disposal), helped him to gain confidence through play. Marley has since become the king of the yard and Clarence is still the happiest dog we've ever seen. Miss MoneyPenny, our fourth, came to us from a couple in Brooklyn who had no time for her, but we think she receives plenty of attention here. Problem dogs? We think not! They're our little bundles of joy. *-Fred & Claudia Fridriksson*

Cat's Best Friend: We thought Bella, our anti-social cat, needed a doggie friend to help her come out of her shell, so we invited Max, a 4-year-old Chihuahua-mix, over for dinner one night with his foster parents. It was an experiment to say the least, but Max immediately captivated Bella with his aloofness. His sweet, innocent, affection then won us all over, so Max never left. Our dog and cat are now best friends, always chasing each other around the house. Sometimes Bella stalks Max, suddenly pouncing on him when he's least expecting it, which incites another wonderful round of play. Max's presence in our lives has made Bella much happier and friendlier to people and animals alike—the transformation is pure magic. *-Sabrina Wilkerson & Jonathan Edmett*

Miracle Money

Lela and Gordi were abandoned in an apartment building in New York City. A dear friend e-mailed her Chihuahua Meetup Group (in which I take part) for emergency help in recovering and fostering the two abandoned dogs, and I responded. When we arrived at the apartment building, Lela had a large, golf ball-sized lump protruding from her belly, which we were not expecting. My friend was going to take Lela and our family Gordi, but after observing Lela closely, we decided I should foster both.

I immediately took the dogs in to see my vet, who diagnosed Lela with several hernias needing to be surgically repaired. Apparently she had been spayed, the wound opened, and her former owners had not returned her to the vet for treatment. This poor girl was in great pain, and I was worried sick. Because I wasn't officially fostering her for a rescue organization, I had to come up with funds for Lela's surgery on my own. I decided I would put it on my credit card if I had to because I was not going to let this little girl suffer further.

I prayed for a miracle, and in the two days between Lela's first vet visit and the next one where we were going to schedule her surgery, Vanessa, who happens to be a vet tech, stopped by to look at another foster I had. She photographed Lela, and unbeknownst to me, texted the pictures to Dr. Gil, the veterinarian for whom she works. We continued discussing the lil' fella she came to adopt, and as I was getting his things together to go home with her, she asked me if she could take Lela to Dr. Gil for surgery. I was shocked at the offer and further surprised when she said that he would do it for $5.25. Thinking I had misheard her, I asked if she meant $525.00, which would even have been a bargain. She double-checked with Dr. Gil, and again came back with *five dollars and twenty-five cents!*

To make a long story short, Lela had her surgery, and while she still needs two additional surgeries, she is much more comfortable. Vanessa decided to foster her because she could give her special care. As for Gordi, he has been neutered and has found his forever family. I believe those of us involved in this particular rescue were brought together for a reason—my prayers were answered and a miracle received. Thank you Vanessa and Dr. Gil Stanzione, DVM!

 *Janie O'Halloran-Chirieleison*

The Ferocious Flower

I was at the vet with one of our pets, when the tech mentioned two Chihuahuas at the pound. The pair's family had packed up, moved, and left them wandering the streets to fend for themselves. The younger and more petite dog was immediately adopted, but Lilly, a larger, portlier dog was left behind in a cage she clearly disliked.

I had wanted another Chi, so we went to visit Lilly, who stood barking ferociously in her cage. I had called earlier to say we were coming, and the employee I spoke with had warned me about the barking. She said Lilly wasn't vicious and advised me to tell the attendant on duty that Lilly would be fine outside of her cage. The shelter worker was right, and once she had been removed from her cage, Lilly relaxed. We felt sorry for Lilly, fearing no one else would take her, so we adopted her. It wasn't love at first sight, but at least she would have a home.

I didn't see Lilly again until I picked her up from her spay, and I had no idea what to expect. I'm a little afraid of dogs and was relieved when she let me carry her without snapping at me. She must have known she was my dog because when my husband arrived home that night, she barked at him and acted protective of me, even though we had both met her together the first time. While to me the barking was equally scary and endearing, my husband didn't let it bother him, and they quickly became friends.

Lilly wasn't really my idea of a Chi. I was used to a petite, gentle, five-pound Chihuahua and our cats. At 12 pounds Lilly was the miniature version of my husband's childhood dog, Baby, a Dachshund/Welsh Corgi mix. Although according to our vet, Lilly was a purebred Chihuahua, the two looked very similar.

On her first day in our home, I put Lilly in the guest room when I went out. I thought that would keep her out of trouble, but she promptly dug through the rug and chewed through a corner of the door. Subsequent attempts to deter her from this behavior using baby gates failed because she chewed through them, too. After some research I learned that Lilly had *severe separation anxiety*. I hadn't heard of it at the time, but it turned out that like many dogs who have come from a situation like Lilly's, the stress of being left alone caused Lilly to behave badly. We combated her fears by occupying her while she was alone, giving her puzzle toys she could push around to release one dry food pellet at a time. We also plugged in an electric pheromone-releasing gadget (like a Glade plug-in), which is purported to have a calming effect on dogs. Lilly responded positively, and her undesirable behaviors subsided.

A week after we adopted Lilly, I took her with me to the transfer station to drop off some recyclables. When I wasn't looking, she extricated herself from her car harness and ran between the large recycling receptacles. We both had bad knees, but hers appeared not to hinder her ability to remain out of my reach for quite some time before I finally caught her. The worker at the station must have thought I was loony as he watched me try to chase down my little dog.

Lilly was an alpha female, a junkyard-type dog. She was the enforcer, the sheriff who kept the peace. She didn't like any kind of tomfoolery, and if the cats were playing or fighting, Lilly would bark at them and get into the middle of things. If our non-dominant Boston Terrier sisters were play-fighting, Lilly would carry on until they stopped, too.

Lilly became friends with Faith, the cat we had adopted a month before Lilly came to live with us. She would charge at Faith, but Faith had known a dog in her previous home and knew not to run. Lilly would be forced to stop in her tracks, and they would sometimes end the day by snuggling up together in Lilly's bed.

Lilly may have been sweet to our cat, but with strangers she was ferocious. On one occasion I was sure she was going to bite the furnace serviceman and his assistant. Some trainers say that if you yell at a barking dog, the dog believes you are joining in, and this encourages him/her to continue threatening. The solution that worked for us was to instead give Lilly treats when she was barking, thus turning a negative experience into a positive one. With her love of food, it didn't take Lilly long to catch on. She quickly began only barking at strangers to get treats, not because she was hostile.

Lilly's tastes were more pedestrian than that of my princess Chi. The only time she ever bit me was when we were fighting over a kitty "bon bon" she had stolen from the litter box. She bit me, I punched her, and we were both sorry. For some unknown reason, I wasn't a bit afraid of her in that instance.

But I think the most memorable day with Lilly was when I took her out for a walk in her dog stroller (her knees were too bad to walk very far) along with our two timid Boston Terriers, and Jeff, a Collie-mix, had apparently decided not to let us pass. Cesar Millan, the television *Dog Whisperer*, advises, "No talk, no touch, no eye contact," in these situations, so I kept my eyes down and just tried to walk past. He snarled and growled from the opposite side of the street, and my two Boston sisters immediately cowered. One slipped out of her harness, and as I fumbled nervously to put it back on, Lilly gave Jeff a piece of her mind. She faced him head on and snarled, making him back off and quiet down a bit. I got the Boston's harness back on, and we victoriously continued on our way. I still laugh when looking back on that moment because my little Lilly was able to dominate the terrifying bigger dog.

Lilly was loyal and fearless. I have no doubt that she would've given her life to protect me, although fortunately no such circumstance emerged. It took me a while to warm up to her and get over my fears, but Lilly definitely worked her way into my heart over time.

 *Raffaela Dwyer*

She Seized Our Hearts

Shannon, a little, eight-year-old, buff-colored Chihuahua, came to me in the most roundabout way. I have a small grooming shop and people often look to me to find great homes for abandoned dogs, cats, and any other animal, for that matter. One of my clients was at her vet when she overheard a man say his wife was having a baby, and he wanted his dog, Shannon, put down. After the man left, my client asked the vet if she could have Shannon. The vet agreed, and she took the dog home, only to find out she was allowed just one pet in her condo unit.

After giving Shannon away, the dog was passed through four other homes, which devastated my client. She called me for help, and I told her I would take Shannon and find her a suitable forever home. By the time I received her, poor little Shannon was sad, nervous, and shaking. She didn't know where she belonged, and it broke my heart.

She continued drooling and shaking when I caged her at my shop, so I took her outside and put her in the grass where she proceeded to flop over like a fish out of water. I knew the vet, so I took Shannon over to see him. He didn't remember her until his office manager reminded him that Shannon was the dog whom he had given to my client. He asked me to put her on the floor, and again she flopped around. The vet told me Shannon was having a seizure and gave me some pills to administer. Now I knew why no one wanted her—they couldn't be bothered with her problems.

At home Shannon's seizures lasted 45 to 90 minutes, until we discovered that a soft blanket and sweet voice could reduce them to only 15. A baby gate allowed Shannon to have the run of a quiet, peaceful part of my home, and her seizures were finally under control. This dog, who was 100% love, stole our hearts, so we decided her forever home would be with us. Shannon loved to play with my daughters, and even though she only weighed nine pounds, she bossed around our other dogs.

At the age of 15, Shannon developed eye problems, requiring that both eyes be removed. When I picked her up from the eye doctor's, even though she couldn't see me, Shannon seemed happy. She kissed me, and her little tail wagged as fast as it could. I had been so worried about the surgery because of Shannon's age, but instead of feeling sorry for herself, Shannon ran around just like she had before the eye removal. If she bumped into a flower or a bush, she would turn around and go the other way, just like a little robot. She was still sweet and cute and our bond became even stronger.

Why Shannon loved people after how they had mistreated her is still mind boggling to me. Shame on the man who wanted her put down and on the other people who hadn't taken the time to get to know her. I guess I should be glad, though, because she was a sweet, little girl, and we felt blessed to have her as a part of our family.

At 16, eight wonderful years after we met her, Shannon passed away in her little blanket, knowing that she was loved.

 *Holly Allen*

Miniature Marvel

When I began fostering Nala, she was underweight, scared, and dragging herself around by her front paws. The Arizona Humane Society veterinarians said she either had fused bones or a broken back, and they feared her disability was permanent. Our rescue's vet had a different perspective, giving Nala the benefit of the doubt that her paralysis was caused by swelling. The vet prescribed *prednisone*, a steroid used to reduce swelling, and we left his office surprised and only slightly hopeful—after all, she had already been lame for so long. Her back legs were atrophying, and the idea that her problem could be something as simple as swelling seemed highly unlikely.

As the days wore on, I found Nala to be loving, trusting, and sweet, and I wanted her to have as normal a life as possible. I gathered information on doggie wheelchairs, and we religiously gave Nala her pills, all the while feeling like we were really just humoring the vet. We focused on providing Nala with the love she deserved and appreciating her for who she was, exactly as she was.

Two weeks into her medication, we noticed a miracle. Though she was a bit wobbly, Nala was clearly trying to stand on all fours. We were delighted when I opened the door for a potty break, and Nala clumsily followed! From then on out, she'd occasionally lose her balance, but she'd get right back up and walk some more.

By the third week, she was walking and building up strength, and after a couple of months, Nala was almost completely healed, with only a slight limp remaining. She was adopted by a wonderful, single, work-at-home woman, who chose Nala as her one and only pet. When she sends me updates around the holidays with pictures of Nala happily sitting in a comfy chair, I couldn't be more proud.

This little girl came into my home with everything wrong but a determination to keep going, and she left me by running into the arms of her new mom, with the promise of bright new life! Is Nala a miracle dog? I'd say so.

 *Stacey Somer*

Working Like a Dog

It was my first day as communications coordinator of an international sandwich chain, and the work was already revolting. After nine months of unemployment and food stamps, I took the first job I was offered. All new hires were required to work in one of their restaurants for up to three weeks, regardless of their positions, so despite being a Jewish vegetarian, I spent my first day slicing and sorting ham. Then, after my three-week stint *serving* meat, I was to sit in a cubicle doing mental gymnastics to *promote* it. I had abandoned my principles for the almighty dollar. Ayn Rand turned over in her grave.

At home I attempted to scrub off the meat, grease, and my sullied values in a scalding shower before surfing the Internet in hopes of finding a way out. My love of animals inevitably took me to Colorado animal rescue websites, and though I didn't find myself a job, I might have done one better. Upon seeing an ad on the Boulder Humane Society website that inquired as to whether my pet was a star, a smile slowly crept across my face. I turned to my Chihuahua/Affenpinscher mix, Lyric, and asked, "Wanna be famous, little girl?" In response she cocked her tiny black head to the side quizzically and wagged her tail.

The ad was referring to the Boulder Dinner Theatre's quest to find an appropriate dog to play Toto in their four-month production of "The Wizard of Oz," and the audition was in two weeks. I called my parents and friends, asking them if they thought she could pass as a male Toto dog from the 1930s. I examined her round head, expressive brown eyes, long lashes, and pert little snout. From the dainty way she reluctantly lifted one paw when I walked her in the rain to the way she crossed her paws in front of her when she slept, she seemed about as butch as Vivien Leigh in *Gone with the Wind*. Could she really impersonate a male dog? I decided to let the PetSmart grooming department increase her casting odds with a simple Cairn Terrier cut.

We arrived at the Boulder Dinner Theatre lobby, and as soon as we saw the director, I immediately recalled the sting of rejection. Over the years I had sent him several demo vocal CDs in an attempt to join his regular adult cast. He shook my hand as if he didn't remember me and offered Lyric a cursory pat on the head. Other dogs and their owners arrived soon thereafter, most entirely wrong for the part.

A trainer from the Boulder Humane Society walked in and recognized Lyric and me from her "beginner," "advanced," and "tricks" classes. She and I nodded and smiled at one another.

A white, curly-haired mutt sniffed a potted plant and lifted his leg, and just as I began to feel superior, Lyric toddled over and added her own yellow brick road. As an employee rushed over with paper napkins to remove the mess, I covered my face with my hands. When I peeked through my fingers, Lyric looked inexplicably thrilled with her accomplishment.

The theater director looked on as the Humane Society trainer asked each dog to perform basic commands. The director said he was concerned about the size of all of the dogs except for a black Cocker Spaniel and Lyric. To help Lyric win the part, I asked if I could demonstrate how well she responds to both my verbal commands and hand signals. After Lyric was finished, the director clapped his hands and praised her as "brilliant."

The Cocker Spaniel was deemed equally as "Toto" as Lyric, so both dogs got the part. We were told that each dog would do three or four shows per week for four months, earning an impressive $40 per show. Our dogs would be independent contractors, but we would have to complete the government paperwork in our own names since canines lack social security numbers. The director offered us days and times when we could come in and go over scene blocking with our dogs on stage.

Due to a scheduling conflict, I was unable to bring Lyric to her first full-cast rehearsal and instead had to ask one of the stagehands to pick her up. Later that night, I received a call from an absolutely ebullient Dinner Theater director, telling me that Lyric had amazing instincts as an actor—she even sat and placed her paw consolingly onto Dorothy's arm as she sang *Somewhere over the Rainbow*. He said that the other cast members watched and cried, and after Mrs. Gulch accused Toto of being vicious, Lyric deadpanned at the audience with the cutest, pleading expression. The director then asked me if Lyric could play the part of Toto for the entire run of the show (now five-months), seven shows per week with none on Monday and two on Sunday. She would be the only cast member without an understudy because the Cocker Spaniel apparently didn't take direction very well. In addition to her checks, Lyric was to be paid in prime rib and doting attention from the cast, and the stagehands would take turns picking her up from my home on days when I worked late—I wouldn't even need to be there. After a twinge of professional jealousy, I said yes and prayed Lyric wouldn't get overwhelmed.

Though my job was filled with gossipy coworkers, mind-numbing busywork, and countless ethical dilemmas, I cheered myself by counting the minutes until I could bring Lyric to her next rehearsal. Finally opening night came, and my boyfriend and I held our breath as orchestral music began and hundreds of people took their seats. We opened our programs, and to our delight, Lyric's headshot was in the playbill along with the human cast members. The lights dimmed, and the young woman playing Dorothy arrived onstage, holding my baby girl in such a way as to conceal her eight nipples. I heard the audience offer a collective, "Awwww," as I turned to a woman next to me and said,

"That's my dog up there!" She smiled condescendingly and announced that her son was in the lollipop guild. *Whatever.*

Soon "Dorothy" began to sing an introductory part of "Somewhere over the Rainbow" that I had never heard before. The lyrics reminded me of my dismal career path versus Lyric's new opportunity, and as I watched the first act, I realized just how important Lyric's role in this musical was. In case you're not familiar with it, the story progresses as follows:

Dorothy runs away from Mrs. Gulch because the old woman threatens to have her dog, Toto, put down for biting her leg. Dorothy is angry at her aunt and the farm staff for not defending Toto against these allegations and certain death. While on the lam, Dorothy sings to Toto of a place where she is understood and her dog would be safe.

In context, this famous song is really a musical ode to the human-animal bond.

As the months progressed, theater reviewers from six local newspapers came to see the show and offer their opinions of the production. Reviews ranged from lukewarm to positive, but without exception, every publication mentioned Lyric by name in absolutely glowing terms.

I saw the show at least 50 times that summer and found a new life lesson in it every time. Eventually I brought an ink pad with me and helped Lyric sign "pawtographs" after performances. Children and elderly folks eagerly posed with her to take commemorative photographs. Lyric was clearly making a difference for others.

I, on the other hand, was not. My meat-inundated restaurant experience had long since passed, but my boss had me rewriting documents late into the night in what I eventually learned was an attempt to make me quit. Before Lyric's five-month *Wizard of Oz* run was over, I was unceremoniously fired. Needless to say, Lyric's more than $5,000 family contribution really came in handy. However, what my little girl taught me was even more valuable than the money: Work should be nothing less than tail waggin' fun, and on the rare occasion it's not, remember there's no place like home.

 *Sheryl Bass*

A Little Love: Anecdotes

Scrappy Scruffy: Scruffy, a Chihuahua/Jack Russell mix, was not the trusting type. He only liked having the top of his back touched, and he would bite anyone who touched him elsewhere. As a new, determined foster parent, I thought I could get through to him, but that took much longer than expected. His slow progress made my two kids and I decide to adopt Scruffy ourselves, and within a year he had become my son's best friend, sharing his plush toys and going for walks. Though Scruffy always wanted to eat strangers alive, he became our beloved family member. Of course, he was a difficult dog at times, but had we not given him the chance to thrive we would have missed out on a great companion. -*Jennifer Prentice*

Chi-hund: Putting our 18-year-old Dachshund to sleep was the hardest thing I ever had to do, but I knew Smedlie was ready to go. A few weeks later my friend and her husband flooded me with pictures of a funny, little dog who kind of looked like a Dachshund but *with huge ears that stuck out sideways*! I looked around a little more, but this dog seemed to be the one, and when we met in person, our connection was immediate. Zoe, our sweet, loving, adorable five-year-old, now spends her time burrowing under the covers and sitting with me while I draw. Occasionally she'll look up at me, almost smiling, and make a little noise. I think she's saying, "Thanks Mom, I love you." -*Kathy Taylor Zimmerman*

The Tradition Continues

For a long time now, my dogs and I have been doing hospice and nursing home work, starting with my Shaggy dog. I am a nurse by profession and have worked in the geriatric field for well over 20 years, so this type of volunteering comes naturally for me.

One day the manager of the hospice I work with called and told me about a man in hospice who had died of a disease that had robbed his family of every last penny. His wife was moving into a shelter until she could figure something out, but she had two Chihuahuas and one Maltese who had apparently stayed on the bed with their master until his last breath. They couldn't accompany her to the shelter—could I help?

I was promised the dogs were piddle-pad trained with no behavioral problems, so I agreed to take them in until the lady could better decide what to do. Well, Sparky, one of the Chihuahuas, walked into my house as if he owned the place. He immediately lifted his leg on all available furniture and then came to me for pets. He was about 11 years old, unneutered, certainly *not* piddle-pad trained, and completely unaware that he might be doing something wrong.

At the time, my household consisted of four different groups of dogs: indoor dogs, porch dogs, Grover the dog-run dog, and now my refugees. As you can image, taking everybody out to potty was a nightmare. The porch dogs, Rover and Candy, had to be escorted off the porch to the run in the yard. Then the inside dogs needed walking. Back at the run, Rover and Candy needed walks and then had to be returned to the porch. Grover, a 75-pound, black-and-tan Coonhound in the run, didn't need anything, but he barked incessantly and ran along his fence while all the shuffling was going on.

Grover was a sweetheart and had never shown aggression toward anybody, but Sparky hated his guts. Even on a leash, Sparky would fly down the steps as soon as I opened the door to get to Grover. Many times he almost strangled himself. When we'd arrive at Grover's fence, eight-pound Sparky would stand on his hind legs and bark at the top of his lungs. Grover would normally come out of his house and stand on the other side of the fence, wondering what was going on. Sometimes he would bark, but mostly he would just look at the little dog and drool.

One day as Sparky carried on, Grover's big head came through the homemade cattle-fencing and suddenly had Sparky's top half in his mouth. When he spit the little guy back out, at first I could find no injury at all. Sparky didn't show any sign of even being intimidated, so we continued on our walk as if nothing had happened. Then I noticed a little blood on his neck, which turned out to be a razor-sharp cut halfway around his throat! I could see all the different layers of skin and other tissue and knew this was not good, so off to the vet we went, who said he had never seen a cut like that from a dog. It took eight stitches to close up the gash. So Sparky continued hating Grover until the day that old man died, which is strange because he loves every other dog.

Sparky's original owner took one of the Chihuahuas back, and the little Maltese was adopted to somebody who really needed her and spoiled her rotten. Adopted by me, Sparky became my hot water bottle and my partner in hospice and nursing home work. He gives kisses to anybody who wants them, can't stand not to be picked up, and always has me in his sights. He is fearless and will protect the bigger dogs from whatever "dangers" may threaten.

Since I had him neutered, Sparky's leg-lifting has decreased to tolerable levels. He is now 15 years old and still chasing my much-younger Dachshund around the yard, even beating him at times!

 *Dee Finch*

Circus Clown

As the co-founder of the Canadian Chihuahua Rescue and Transport (CCRT), I have fostered, transported, and met thousands of dogs over the past 10 years. I love them all, and while it's always sad to see foster dogs leave my home for their new "forever" homes, it makes me happy to know I have done something to improve their lives. Believe it or not, in those 10 years, I never seriously considered adopting one of our rescues until the day I met a smiling, overweight, nine-year-old Chihuahua named Melly.

I received a call from the Ottawa Humane Society about a dog who had come in as a stray, and due to some medical issues, they thought it best she be taken into rescue. I picked her up and instantly fell in love with all 20 pounds of her! (She was morbidly obese and desperately needed to go on a diet.) She stayed with me for a few days until she could hitch a ride to her foster home in Elliot Lake, Ontario, 750 km from my home.

Sadly, during Melly's few days with me, my own 14-year-old Chihuahua, Newton, passed away. I was devastated, but this is when my bond with Melly truly began to form. I considered adopting her but thought it better not to make any big decisions while I was grieving so much for Newton.

Melly went to her foster home and lost six pounds in just a couple of months. (Why can't I do that?) I stayed in touch with her foster mom, who sent me regular updates and photos. With each update, I fell more and more in love.

On my birthday I finally realized I was ready for another dog, and that dog had to be Melly. I officially adopted her and made the 7½-hour, one-way drive to pick her up. I couldn't believe it when I saw her—she looked so slim and trim!

I returned to Ottawa the same day (yes, that's 15 hours of driving in one day), and abruptly found out that Melly was petrified of car rides. She cried and whined in the passenger seat, and while calmer in the backseat, she still shook like a leaf and paced a lot. It was a very long 7½ hours, which left me wondering whether I had made the right decision to adopt Melly. Was this nervous behavior a reflection of her true personality?

That wasn't the case, and two years later I can't imagine my life without Melly. She has lost another few pounds, and while she remains a curvy gal, she is in much better shape now. She is such a clown that I tell people she ran away from the circus. Like all dogs, her favorite things are walks and food, and she also enjoys curling up on the ottoman at my feet while I watch TV. She was pretty much housebroken from the moment she came to CCRT, has amazing recall, walks perfectly off-leash, and even does tricks. It boggles my mind that such a well-behaved, trained dog was not claimed at the Humane Society by her owners. Someone obviously loved her very much.

Today her hearing and sight aren't what they used to be and some medical issues are creeping up. She has developed a serious snoring problem that keeps me up all night, but she remains a happy, smiling dog, who loves nothing more than to be in the same room as her momma. Her momma adores and loves her right back.

Melly is a wonderful example of the many, many older dogs in rescue who want nothing more that to find a stable, loving home to call their own.

 *Nathalie C. Houle*

Wiggled Into My Life

November was very difficult. My 15-month-old Lab/ Catahoula mix, Payson, had been diagnosed with *valley fever*, a fungal infection. Regrettably, within two days the medication caused her liver to fail, and she died. And as if I wasn't devastated enough, three days later our 14-year-old Lab/Chow mix, Shadow, collapsed, and I had to make the awful decision to finally help her cross the Rainbow Bridge.

For the first time in my life, I was without a dog. Growing up my father was in the military, and one of my first dogs was a two-pound Chihuahua named Tinker. She was the perfect "portable dog" for our transient lifestyle, and I've always wanted another Chihuahua. With the big dogs gone and my kids off to college, I decided I would finally get my dream dog.

Upon beginning my search, I found many websites inviting me to purchase a teacup Chihuahua. They were all tempting until I learned they could be fronts for puppy mills, commercial breeding facilities that are infamous for mistreating dogs. Not wanting to support the horrific suffering experienced by those unfortunate breeding dogs and their puppies, who are generally weaned too early and sold online and through pet shops, I looked for a rescue. On the Arizona Chihuahua Rescue (AZCR) website, I scrolled through the pictures of currently available fur-babies, but I didn't see anyone who jumped out at me. Then, at the bottom of the page among the "future adoptables," I saw Wiggles, a little, white-ticked boy with floppy ears, stitches, and no front right leg.

Wiggles' history stated that his owner had accidentally stepped on him and broken his right front leg at the elbow when he was three months old. The owner refused to spend the money for the multiple surgeries it would take to fix Wiggles' leg as it grew, and he asked the vet to put him down. Instead, the scrupulous vet called AZCR, and Wiggles was relayed from Tucson to one of their foster families in Phoenix by three different drivers. The next morning his right front leg was removed.

For some reason Wiggles just struck me, and I decided he was the one. But corresponding with his foster mom, Becky, only left me disappointed because it turned out that Wiggles already had someone interested in him. I continued my search for the perfect dog, emailing photos back and forth with my mother in Florida. She would send me a picture of a dog from a breeder, and I would send back Wiggles' photo, the three-legged dog with eyes that bored into my soul. Finally my mom encouraged me to double check with Becky, and I came to find out that Wiggles hadn't been adopted! I put in my application straight away and was approved, so my brother, his girlfriend, and I diligently cleaned my home to prepare for Wiggles' home visit.

Becky and Wiggles came on Sunday at 11:00am. The doorbell rang, and upon seeing them there, I started to cry at the joyful thought of this little soul coming into my life. Becky immediately handed Wiggles to me, and he gently put his head on my shoulder, as if to say, "It's going to be okay; I am here now."

We renamed him Lefty, which seemed fitting, and we quickly realized he can do anything a "four-legger" can. He runs and plays, jumps on the couch, and goes in and out of the doggy door. He doesn't let a little thing like a missing leg interfere with his life.

I have medical issues, and I call Lefty my magic dog because he alerts me when I am about to have an episode. He now acts as my service dog, going everywhere with me. Lefty has since helped me foster 21 dogs for AZCR, always welcoming the next foster with a tail wag and a lick. He attends many AZCR events, serving as an ambassador for rescued animals. He's proof that "secondhand" dogs have something to give and should never be thrown away.

Though you may think that I saved Lefty, you would be wrong. In truth it is Lefty who saved me.

 *Sandra Mundt*

Resilience

The first time I saw the tiny fellow he was no more than a shell of what had once been a dog. Even though I'd been a dog rescuer for years and thought I'd seen it all, his condition was shocking. His eyes were oozing with infection, most of his hair and teeth were missing, his nails were growing into the pads of his feet, and he was absolutely crawling with fleas. Skeletal, shivering, and nearly too weak to stand, he'd been dumped in the pound to die.

He was so frail and helpless that leaving him there was not an option, so I brought him home. I could only assume the little guy had never been given a proper name and was probably known simply by the lovely green numbers tattooed in his ear. I decided to call him Tommy. His tattoo and deplorable health tipped me off that my Tommy was a puppy mill throwaway. It appeared his previous owner, a person who obviously bred dogs for money without a care for their health and happiness, had deemed him too old to be useful any longer. I suppose I should've been grateful he hadn't just been drowned, shot, or left in a cage to starve like they sometimes do with their "useless" dogs. At least they'd taken him to the pound, right?

I couldn't tell with any certainty how old he was, but Tommy appeared to be about 15. Considering his advanced age and poor physical health, I felt the best I could hope for was to give him a soft landing—a sweet and memorable place to die. What I couldn't have possibly known was that I would be utterly and completely taken in by this tiny package, but it quickly became very clear that I needed to give him much more. He deserved a sweet and memorable place *to live*! And before I realized it, Tommy began to teach me a thing or two about life and the resiliency of spirit.

The first few weeks with him were heartbreaking. I'd never met a dog so utterly void of emotion. If the eyes are the window to the soul, I'd have been forced to believe he had none. His days consisted of sleeping or staring into a corner, avoiding contact with me if at all possible. He refused to look at me when I held him and his body would stiffen as if he were steeling himself against whatever punishment was to come. As the months passed, I began to think he was just too damaged to ever open up. That he would remain forever locked in the prison of his past abuses.

Physically, Tommy improved dramatically with just a bit of basic care. He was up to a whopping *four pounds* in a matter of weeks. His hair quickly grew back, becoming soft and shiny, and he seemed less anxious, even able to interact with my other dogs. But he continued to be completely terrified of me. Occasionally I would be fortunate enough to enter the room unnoticed and could quietly steal a moment when he appeared to be happy and carefree. Those moments were always fleeting, though, because he would shut down again the instant he realized I was watching. Sadly, I resigned myself to the fact that Tommy no longer had the ability to bond with people. I believed that his years without human affection had so severely scarred him that the window of opportunity had long since closed.

And then, suddenly, one day he wagged his tail—*at me*! It was just a tiny wag, but I saw it. The following days brought more breakthroughs, as Tommy began to come toward me whenever I entered the room. Not all the way to me, of course, but close enough to say, "I missed you, and I'm so glad you're home." Slowly but surely, I was being accepted, and each breakthrough felt like victory.

Three years have passed since then, and although he's clearly an old man, Tommy can still light up the room. Now, as I watch him romp and play with an expression of pure joy on his face, I see that the spirit can indeed be healed. When he runs to me to be held and then relaxes in my arms, I know that trust can be restored. When he sleeps peacefully and soundly on my lap, I realize that all fears, great and small, can be conquered. And when he basks in the sun on a warm summer day, I remember that we all should cling tightly to the simple pleasures of life.

As I put these words on paper, Tommy snores quietly on my lap, and I feel very blessed. He's a beautiful, little soul and I'm fortunate to have found him. To think of this little one suffering day after day for years in a small wire cage, with no one to love him, makes my heart ache with a longing for the life he deserved and should have always had. Nevertheless, I believe that my Tommy has finally let go of the past and carries with him only memories of love and happy days. Watching his transformation has been an experience I'll cherish for the rest of my life. He has no idea what a gift he's been to me.

It took almost a lifetime, but my tiny Tommy finally found his very own place to belong—forever in my heart and in my home.

 *Donna Little*

Reduce, Reuse, Recycle

There she lay, curled in a tight ball, shaking in the cold cement corner. The wire fence kept me from rushing in and rescuing her, but I wanted terribly to give her what I felt she lacked—love, warmth, a proper home. I couldn't help but worry whether her short, tortured life had left her aggressive, but I'm not so risk adverse that I wouldn't try. So I went to ask for the gate to be opened and a chance to search her soul.

The shelter worker placed her hand on her hip, checking for keys. "Yep, got um," she grinned. After retrieving a blue and yellow, frayed leash with a noose at one end, she led me towards building C, Kennel #36: Females. I asked questions as we walked, hoping to find out that little creature wasn't as bad off as I was imagining. "How long has she been here?" I inquired.

"Quite a while. Today is her last day," the emotionally-conditioned worker replied.

"Has anyone requested to see her?" I asked as my heart begged for a yes.

"Nope, you are the first," she answered.

"How could anyone avoid her need for love?" I thought out loud.

"It's easy for some. Many people just see something somebody threw out." she griped.

We arrived at enclosure #36 to the little dog still curled up tightly with her head tucked deep inside her body. As the frightened occupant heard the *CLANK* of her gate unlocking, she sprinted out the small door opposite us. "Shoot!" the worker cursed. "I hate when they do that!"

While the worker reluctantly walked around to the outside kennel to herd the dog back in, I scolded myself for even being there. Suddenly a white flash crossed the gray kennel floor, accompanied by a loud *BANG* as the outside door slammed shut to trap her inside. "We got her now!" the worker victoriously yelled.

Without hesitation the worker stepped into the kennel, noosed the dog's rigid form, snatched her up, and headed for the "getting acquainted" area. This area consisted of a chain link fence enclosing two benches, a water bowl, and nowhere to hide. The worker placed the dog on the cement slab, and the fearful prisoner froze. I squatted beside her and crisscrossed my legs on the cold floor, wondering what could have happened to this small creature to suspend her in this statue-like posture. Didn't she realize I was here to help?

This dog weighed perhaps a pound, on a frame that ought to weigh seven. Her hairless skin, tinted a pasty pink, displayed random black patches and spots. The imbalance of one black, folded-down ear and an erect, white, speckled ear gave her an uneven look. A tuft of white hair centered between her ears reminded me of an 80's hairstyle.

Due to a lack of human physical care, her purpose in life had been reduced to an incubator for parasites. I wanted so badly to cradle her and show her kindness, but instead I sat there motionless, eyes fixed, watching her skin crawl with parasitic life, keeping my distance. I blinked back the tears as I questioned how anyone could be so cruel. Then and there I made the decision to foster her—no, to *recycle* her, a thought that made me smile.

The fostering papers were completed, the $85 fee paid, and she was given a dip to rid her of most of the parasites. I packaged her in my towel and headed for the van. Before arriving home we stopped at the vet—I didn't want to unintentionally bring any diseases home to my first two rescues. The visit revealed malnutrition, *anemia* (a condition where the body does not have enough healthy red blood cells), depression, *Rocky Mountain spotted fever* (an infectious disease caused by tick bites), and *ehrlichiosis* (a disease of the white blood cells which is also transmitted by ticks). "You have a lot of work ahead of you. But she seems like a worthy dog," Dr. Boone commented.

At home my sons chose the name Zoe out of a baby book for her. I fixed her a bed in the bottom half of a small, collapsible crate, tied her loosely to the table leg nearby, and left her to get accustomed to her new surroundings. She remained motionless, head buried deep in the bed, afraid to make eye contact.

As the weeks went by, our family continued our normal lives around her. We decided that each time someone passed her they should pat her gently on the head and say, "Good girl." Zoe would only venture from her hidden position when no one was watching. Sensing we had left the room, she would sneak around to find us but would run back to the safety of her bed once we noticed her. She desperately longed to be with us but didn't understand how to do so. Unable to walk on a leash the conventional way, I clipped her to Harley, my rescue Chihuahua, and she followed him as we walked.

After months of creative "recycling" techniques, Zoe's trust in humans was restored. By that time our love for her had grown very strong and giving her up for adoption, as planned, became impossible. So I headed back to the shelter to sign the adoption papers and make Zoe a permanent member of our family.

Zoe is now a well-adjusted, loving, dedicated, funny, outgoing dog. She spends her days following mom around the house and playing with friends, her evenings sitting on dad's lap, sharing sunflower seeds and watching television, and her nights snoring in a soft bed. She competed in the Amarillo Muttfest "Queen Mutt" and "Waggin'est Tail" contests, taking the title in both. I wonder what life would be like had I not given her a second chance. All I know is that I am very glad I did. Why buy new, when recycled dogs have so much character?

I have many people ask me where they can get a dog like Zoe. I tell them, "There are many animals just like her in shelters across the states, waiting for someone to give them another chance at life." I only wish that more people would go into shelters and take some time to penetrate the shells of "used and discarded" animals. These animals crave love and human companionship but sometimes just need to be taught how to access it. Though some dogs take longer than others, most shelter animals do not require as much time and patience as we had to give Zoe. They all need love, discipline, and guidance, and most are just thrilled with becoming a loved and cherished family member.

The moral of the story is this: Before you spend that large sum of money on a "new" pet, first walk through your local shelter. Take your time, and truly search the souls of the animals waiting on death row. Who knows, you might find yourself to be a happy recycler, too!

 *Leslie Holman*

Nikki's Gingerbread Man Dog Treats

My dogs, Chico, Manny, and Bebe, love homemade Gingerbread Man dog treats, and I'm sure your Chi will, too! You'll need cookie cutters (gingerbread men or any other fun shapes) and the following ingredients:

4 cups whole wheat flour
1-1/2 cup old-fashioned oats
3 tablespoons powdered ginger
1 tablespoon powdered garlic
4 large eggs
1 cup molasses
2/3 Cup Vegetable Oil
1/4 Cup Honey

Instructions:

1. Preheat oven to 325 degrees.

2. Place dry ingredients (flour, oats, ginger, and garlic) in a medium to large mixing bowl and blend with a whisk.

3. Add eggs, molasses, vegetable oil, and honey, and mix until blended. (I use my clean hands to mix it all together until it the dough is completely blended.)

4. Roll out sections of dough to ¼ inch thick, and use cookie cutters to cut out your cookies.

5. Place cut-outs on cookie sheets, making sure they aren't touching each other.

6. Continue to take sections of dough, rolling, and cutting out pieces until you use it all up. (This recipe makes 40-50 gingerbread man-sized treats.)

7. Bake at 325 degrees for 20-30 minutes (slightly hotter and longer if you live at a high altitude).

8. Let the treats cool at least a half an hour or until they are not hot to the touch before giving to your dogs.

9. Give them to your dogs and watch them enjoy!

 Note: When you take your cookies out of the oven, they may feel slightly soft to the touch, but they will harden as they cool down.

 Nikki Figular, obsessivechihuahuadisorder.com

About Happy Tails Books™

Happy Tails Books™ was created to help support animal rescue efforts by showcasing the love, happiness, and joy adopted dogs have to offer. With the help of animal rescue groups, stories are submitted by people who have adopted dogs, and then Happy Tails Books™ compiles them into breed-specific books. These books serve not only to entertain, but also to educate readers about dog adoption and the characteristics of each specific type of dog. Happy Tails Books™ donates a significant portion of proceeds back to the rescue groups who help gather stories for the books.

 Happy Tails Books™ To submit a story or learn about other books Happy Tails Books™ publishes, please visit our website at http://happytailsbooks.com.

We're Writing Books About Your Favorite Dogs!

Schnauzer Chihuahua Golden Retriever **PUG**

DACHSHUND German Shepherd Collie **Boxer**

Labrador Retriever Husky Beagle ALL AMERICAN

Border Collie Pit Bull Terrier Shih Tzu Miniature Pinscher

Chow Chow Australian Shepherd Rottweiler Greyhound

Boston Terrier Jack Russell Poodle Cocker Spaniel

GREAT DANE Doberman Pinscher Yorkie **SHEEPDOG**

ST. BERNARD Pointer Blue Heeler

Find Them at Happytailsbooks.com!

Make your dog famous!

Do you have a great story about your adopted dog? We are looking for stories, poems, and even your dog's favorite recipes to include on our website and in upcoming books! Please visit the website below for story guidelines and submission instructions. **http://happytailsbooks.com/submit.htm**